SHORT CUTS

INTRODUCTIONS TO FILM STUDIES

QUEER CINEMA

SCHOOLGIRLS, VAMPIRES AND GAY COWBOYS

BARBARA MENNEL

WALLFLOWER

LONDON and NEW YORK

A Wallflower Press Book
Published by
Columbia University Press
Publishers Since 1893
New York • Chichester, West Sussex
cup.columbia.edu

Wallflower Press® is a registered trademark of Columbia University Press

Cataloging-in-Publication Data is available from the Library of Congress

ISBN 978-0-231-16313-2 (pbk.)
ISBN 978-0-231-85020-9 (e-book)

Book and cover design: Rob Bowden Design
Cover image: *Brokeback Mountain* (2005)

CONTENTS

ACKNOWLEDGEMENTS

I am indebted to Yoram Allon at Wallflower Press for supporting this project, part of his general invigoration of Film Studies. I thank the Photo Archive of the Deutsche Kinemathek for permission to reprint the stills in this volume and Peter Latta for his kind and generous help. Amy Ongiri, Jodi Schorb, Kim Emery and Katherine Baker provided great company, alternating between sentimental memories, silly commentaries and engaging critical debates while watching lesbian cinema and television in the early stages of this project. Katrin Sieg put together a panel on 'Queer Film in Contemporary Europe' at the German Studies Association where I profited from discussions with B. Venkat Mani and Randall Halle. I have had the privilege to learn from Katrin Sieg's insights into queer theory and its pitfalls over the years. Jeffrey S. Adler spent many a night watching the films that make up this book, accompanied by Lizzie – a dog with a peculiar taste for queer cinema. I am particularly indebted to those who have taken the time to read individual chapters and provide extensive, productive and smart feedback: Jeffrey S. Adler, Kim Emery, Sabine Hake, Kenneth Kidd, Amy Ongiri, Brad Prager, Jeffrey Schneider and Jodi Schorb. A special shout-out goes to founding writing-club members Kenneth Kidd and Jodi Schorb for making writing fun!

INTRODUCTION

Schoolgirls, vampires and gay cowboys are the heroes of this book. The former – schoolgirls and vampires – emerged in German films as ciphers of queer desire at the beginning of the twentieth century, while the latter – Ang Lee's gay cowboys – queer the most manly of men and symbolise the presence of gays and lesbians in contemporary Hollywood. It is from the moment of omnipresence of gays and lesbians on television and in the movies – as main characters, their relatives, neighbours and best friends – that we return to a past when a character could be discredited as 'queer' by a calling card that smelled of lavender, as Joel Cairo famously was in John Huston's *The Maltese Falcon* (1941). The tragic and monstrous queer fore-runners of their contemporary well-adjusted gay and lesbian counterparts populate the history of queer cinema and allow us to trace its different incarnations. This book brings together important moments, periods and turning points that add up to a history of queer film.

Queer Cinema thus goes beyond describing gay and lesbian films to participate in a larger project of queer Film Studies: an archeology of an alternative cinematic aesthetics organised around non-normative desires. 'Queer' exceeds the notions of gay and lesbian identities that emerged in Paris, London, New York and Berlin at the beginning of the twentieth century. For some, 'gay' and 'lesbian' are descriptive terms that capture socially lived experience, while for others they constitute the political pro-gramme of declaring one's gay or lesbian identity. Naming and publicly embodying a different desire transcends compulsory heterosexuality and demands rights to diverse sexual, erotic and affective relationships and gendered embodiments.

Sexuality and gender played a central role in the history of film, even before feature-length narrative films developed, because the medium engages the different pleasures of looking and being looked at: voyeurism and exhibitionism. Cinema is deeply ingrained with heterosexual and gendered assumptions, which also shape the vocabulary and methodologies of Film Studies. The important scholar of early cinema, Tom Gunning argues that before 1906, short films constituted an 'exhibitionist cinema', celebrating 'its ability to show something', which he contrasts to 'the voyeuristic aspect of narrative cinema', which developed later (1990: 57). To illustrate his case, Gunning points to *The Bride Retires* (1902): 'A woman undresses for bed while her new husband peers at her from behind the screen. However, it is to the camera and the audience that the bride addresses her erotic striptease, winking at us as she faces us, smiling in erotic display' (ibid.). The concepts of voyeurism and exhibitionism are shaped by gendered assumptions about heterosexual male voyeurs and female exhibitionists: the pairing of man and woman as husband and wife inscribes the structure of looking and being looked at, in which masculinity is associated with a desire to look and femininity with a desire to be looked at, bound together by the heterosexual contract (see Mulvey 1988a).

If movies show the stuff that dreams are made of, queer films can set the stage for fantasies that are structured by same-sex attraction: this time, when the princess kisses the frog, the repulsive animal might turn out to be a girl. Generally queer film promises to tell stories about gays and lesbians who negotiate events typical for their lived collective experiences: alienated youth and unrequited crushes; sexual awakening and coming out; the trials and tribulations of gay and lesbian communities. By representing defamed desires and allowing audiences an affective engagement with them, queer film is inherently political.

Yet, while this description captures the contemporary connotations of gay and lesbian films, it cannot provide a comprehensive approach to earlier queer culture – and its presence in film. According to historian George Chauncey's work on New York City between 1890 and 1940, the taboos against non-normative sexualities and genders led gays and lesbians to develop a 'highly sophisticated system of subcultural codes' for recognising and communicating with each other (1994: 4). Because gays and lesbians brought these codes to the making and watching of movies, queer cinema also includes the traces of a hidden presence, readable in its imprints, inferences, codes, subtexts and styles.

This book, then, suggests that the term 'queer' enables a productive intervention into the visual representation of same-sex desire and the history of cinema. 'Queer' encapsulates 'perverse' sexualities without fixing them into specific identities and can therefore capture different configurations of cinematic representation and non-normative desire, even regarding films that do not include explicit representations of homosexuality. 'Queer' has come to function as a short-hand, an umbrella term signifying a range of non-normative sexual and gender identities, including gay, lesbian, bisexual, cross-dressing, transvestite, transgender, transsexual, intersex, effeminate men and butch women.

This list, however, does not capture queer's deconstructive dimension. Queer theorist Judith Butler, in *Gender Trouble* (1990), argues that making identity the basis of political analysis and movement, as in 'women's movement' or 'lesbian activism', presupposes of a coherence that limits the possibilities of expressing subject positions. 'Queer' implies the subversion of gender and sexual identities assumed to be cohesive, while 'gay' and 'lesbian' claims the political productivity of circulating such identities in the public sphere in order to demand equal rights. Since the medium of film lends itself to a realist representation of identity as well as to its artistic deconstruction, both approaches exist in filmic production and reception.

Queer Cinema negotiates possible theoretical conflicts marked by the terms 'gay' and 'lesbian' vis-à-vis 'queer' by framing its discussion in the historical contexts from which those terms emerged in the first place. Descriptors reflect the discursive context of the period that gave birth to them. 'Invert', 'third sex' and 'uranian' emerged in turn-of-the-century sexology only to make their way into the subcultural codes of the Weimar Republic, for example in the phrase 'saucy daddy' [KV, short for *Kesse Vater*] as code for a butch (masculine looking and acting) lesbian (see Zur Nieden 2003). The American mid-century phrase 'a friend of Dorothy', a code of recognition for gay men, presumably was based on a camp reading of Victor Fleming's *The Wizard of Oz* (1939) staring gay icon Judy Garland as Dorothy and as such indicates the importance of film in gay and lesbian subcultures. The terms 'gay' and 'lesbian' are rooted in the homosexual rights movement that emerged from the late 1960s throughout the 1970s. The shorthand 'Stonewall' – referring to bloody riots of drag queens resisting police raids of gay bars in 1969 in New York City – came to stand for a turning point from a subcultural existence that relied on codes of recognition to an 'out' life style that demanded visibility and claimed normalcy. The term 'queer' was appropriated in the political activism around AIDS of the late 1980s and early 1990s. These terms are therefore not mutually exclusive, but instead relate to each other across a historical continuum. Socio-political contexts and intentionality of speakers inflect their meaning.

Thus, this book's methodology and terms reflect a moment in which queer film theory has been consolidated and the gay and lesbian rights movement has achieved some of its goals. 'Gay' and 'lesbian' refers to men-loving-men and women-loving-women. It applies to characters, their sexual desires and political identities, whether explicit or implicit, to films that address them and to self-identified directors, actors and producers. An approach committed to homosexual rights suggests that conventional representation of gays and lesbians in film constitutes societal acceptance and indicates political and social progress. Queer Film Studies, however, proposes that non-normative desire undermines cinematic conventions because the subversion of coherent identity also questions the possibility of its mimetic representation in film. Queer film aesthetics challenges the cinematic conventions based on gender-normative heterosexuality.

Film Studies has witnessed a development from gay and lesbian history to queer theory. Foundational books by Richard Dyer, Vito Russo and Andrea Weiss established gay and lesbian film history, while a contemporary proliferation of theorists and publications constitute Queer Film Studies (discussed in depth in chapter four). A brief example organised around the theoretical approach to cinematic visibility and invisibility illustrates this shift. Film scholar Andrea Weiss (1992) argues that the study of cinema as visual medium is crucial for the representation of lesbians because their oppression has taken the form of enforced invisibility.

Seven years later, Patricia White, a scholar trained in Queer Studies, modifies this argument by suggesting that even though, for example, the Production Code Administration in mid-twentieth-century Hollywood attempted to make lesbianism invisible, individual films nevertheless register effects (1999: xvii). The production code forbad the representation of 'sex perversion' as well as its inference, without naming lesbianism. Yet, as White points out, even the 'motion picture industry practitioners recognised censorship as a set of codes for producing meaning, and particularly sexual meaning, and indeed for producing readings' (1999: 8). She reads

Hollywood films made under the production code to excavate the traces of lesbian desire paradoxically produced by its prohibition.

To capture the changing configurations of politics and aesthetics on the one hand and visibility and invisibility on the other, *Queer Cinema* is organised around five key historical moments. Chapter one discusses films associated with a period of liberation movements for homosexuals and lesbians, the Weimar Republic (1918–33) in Germany. Chapter two is organised around camp as a gay aesthetics, which connected films produced in the Hollywood studio system, B movies, experimental and art film during the 1940s to the early 1970s in the US.

The two decades following the Stonewall Rebellion of 1969 in New York take centre stage in chapter three as a symbolic turning point cast as a collective coming out in films that unapologetically showed gays and lesbians often as positive identification figure in realist settings. The New Queer Cinema of the early 1990s is the topic of chapter four, which describes the radical and highly aestheticised films that often portrayed queers in the margin of past and contemporary societies. New Queer Cinema belonged to a larger political, social and cultural force; while juxtaposed to mainstream cinema, it nevertheless paved the way for the presence of gays and lesbians in conventional films, which is discussed in chapter five. This last chapter examines the wave of gay- and lesbian-themed films targeting general mainstream audiences as well as specifically gay and lesbian moviegoers and addresses the proliferation of international queer cinema. The conclusion suggests that the current hypertext and multi-media environment goes hand in glove with a deconstruction of gender and sexuality, expanding the term queer to include cross-dressing, transgender, transsexual and intersex characters in films and web-based art projects. Taken together, the chapters assembled here retrace the complex interconnections between politics and aesthetics that fueled the filmic developments of what we now call 'queer cinema'.

1   THE ORIGINS OF QUEER CINEMA: SCHOOLGIRLS, VAMPIRES AND CROSS-DRESSERS

Queer figures, from schoolgirls to vampires, populate the films of Germany's Weimar Republic, a period inaugurated by the end of World War One in 1918 and brought to an abrupt and violent end with Hitler's ascendance to power in 1933. During those fifteen turbulent years of Germany's first democracy, gay and lesbian political and social movements thrived, and so did the movie industry. The first explicitly homosexual rights film was made as early as 1919. Richard Oswald's feature-length silent classic *Anders als die Anderen* (*Different from the Others*) narrates a tragic story about homosexual lives ruined by extortion. Toward the end of the period, the box office hit and early sound film, Leontine Sagan's *Mädchen in Uniform* (*Girls in Uniform*) (1931) tells a tale now considered the *Urtext* of the schoolgirl genre, a staple of lesbian film. Homosexuals were everywhere: not just in bars, dance houses and cabarets but also in literature, painting and film. Yet this presence was neither an isolated cultural phenomenon nor an uncontested existence.

The homosexual and women's rights movements and the exploration of the new medium of film were part of larger processes of modernisation in the early twentieth century. Arts movements, such as dada, expressionism and new objectivity, revolutionised literature and painting. The Bauhaus philosophy redefined architecture and interior design with an eye to efficiency and rationalism. Technological innovations led to increased speed in communication, transportation and industrial production. Women received the vote and entered the university and the workforce in record numbers.

Bodies were liberated from stifling traditions with knee-length skirts, nudism and wild dance styles imported from America. The New Woman was flat-chested, cropped her hair and smoked in coffee houses and bars. The modern woman and the modern man were androgynous creatures. The roaring twenties witnessed an explosive sexual and social life for gay men, lesbians, transvestites and those who enjoyed their company.

The politicisation and social visibility of gays and lesbians in the Weimar Republic had its roots in the late nineteenth century. In turn-of-the-century Vienna and London, writers such as Frank Wedekind, Oscar Wilde and Arthur Schnitzler and painters such as Gustav Klimt produced works that were explicitly sexual. During the nineteenth century male homosexuality became both 'extremely public' and, at the same time, linked to secrets (see Sedgwick 1990: 164). Lord Alfred Douglas' famous line in his poem 'Two Loves' (1894), 'I am the love that dare not speak its name', encapsulates the secrecy that was constitutive of homosexuality (see Murray 2000). Nineteenth-century sexology developed a new, scientific language to define and catalogue normative and perverse sexual behaviours and identities. Homosexuality at the turn-of-the-century was a closeted affair and turned into a scandal when made public as when in 1907 journalist Maximilian Harden suggested that General Count Kuno von Moltke, Prince Philipp of Eulenburg and others in the Emperor Wilhelm II's inner circle were homosexuals. They, in turn, charged him with libel, and the trial evolved into a public scandal that lasted two years and ruined the lives of the accused (see Schneider 1997).

But the increasing urbanisation permitted public expression of gay and lesbian identities in the anonymity of cities, turning Berlin of the 1920s into the hotspot of queer culture where the presence of members of the so-called third sex, also called inverts, including gays, lesbians, transsexuals and transvestites, could not be overlooked. Famous bars, such as the 'Mikado' and the 'Eldorado' catered to homosexuals and transvestites, while others, such as the 'Golden Ball', 'Violetta', 'Monbijou' or 'Sappho' served lesbians (see Dobler 2003). Magazines aided lesbians in networking to meet like-minded women, find romance or reflect on politics (see Schoppmann 1996; Dobler 2003). At grand masquerade balls, women dressed as men and men as women.

Social activities overlapped with political ones, split along the lines of gender and the different understanding of homosexuality. By the 1920s,

gays and lesbians could look back on decades of homosexual rights movements and an even longer tradition of understanding homosexuality. Since
the turn of the century the gay 'community' had consisted of two wings:
a political homosexual rights movement that relied on legal and medical
arguments in contrast to groups that favoured homoerotic friendships
between men (see Ivory 2003). Gay rights activist and sexologist Magnus
Hirschfeld and the Scientific-Humanitarian Committee (SHC) represented
the former and continued their work throughout the Weimar Republic.
Hirschfeld considered homosexuality to be inborn, resulting from a person
being born in the wrong body. For example, 'Uranian' ['Urning'] defined a
person with female psyche in a male body. In 1904, the annual assembly
of the SHC was the setting of Anna Rüling's famous speech 'Homosexuality
and the Women's Movement', which proposed the collaboration of the
homosexual rights movement with feminism (see Leidinger 2004). The
other wing of the homosexual movement was embodied by Adolf Brand
who advocated heterosexual marriage accompanied by idealised male/
male relationships, evoking Hellenistic ideals of the 'pedagogic eros'
between older and younger men as a sign of virile masculinity (see Ivory
2003).

The topic of male homosexuality dominated the debates about same-
sex love. Paragraph 175 of the German Criminal Code specifically criminal-
ised 'homosexual activities among men that were similar to penetration'
['beischlafähnlich'] and its abolition was the main goal of the gay rights
movement (see Dobler 2003). While lesbians were equally present in
the subcultural social life, they were less visible in the explicitly political
activism (see Faderman & Eriksson 1980). Women had only been admit-
ted to universities by 1908 and did not fit the 'academic structure' of the
SHC, and since they were also prohibited from political organising in most
German states until 1908, they founded clubs officially registered for social
activities, such as bowling (see Schoppmann 1996).

Films of the period reflect the social presence of gays and lesbians and
the concerns of the homosexual rights movement. *Different from the Others*
advances the agenda of the political gay rights movement in the Weimar
Republic. Other films include gays or lesbians as main characters or as
minor figures or create the possibility of a queer but indeterminate reading. An incomplete list of films that fulfill either of these criteria includes
Richard Oswald's *Das Bildnis des Dorian Gray* (*The Picture of Dorian Gray*)

(1917), *Aus eines Mannes Mädchenjahren* (*A Man's Girlhood*) (1919), Fritz Lang's *Dr. Mabuse, der Spieler* (*Dr. Mabuse: The Gambler*) (1922), Friedrich Wilhelm Murnau's *Nosferatu* (1922), Carl Theodor Dreyer's *Michael* (1924), Nicholas Kaufmann's and Wilhelm Prager's *Wege zu Kraft und Schönheit* (*Ways to Strength and Beauty*) (1925), Alfred Schirokauer's *Der Himmel auf Erden* (*Heaven on Earth*) (1927), William Dieterle's *Geschlecht in Fesseln* (*Sex in Chains*) (1928), Georg Wilhelm Pabst's *Die Büchse der Pandora* (*Pandora's Box*) (1929), Karl Anton's *Der Fall des Generalstabs-Oberst Redl* (*The Case of Colonel Redl*) (1931), Leontine Sagan's *Girls in Uniform* (1931) and Lang's *Das Testament des Dr. Mabuse* (*The Testament of Dr. Mabuse*) (1933).

Weimar Cinema also enjoyed the convention of the so-called 'trouser roles', in which female characters cross-dress as men, such as Ernst Lubitsch's *Ich möchte kein Mann sein* (*I Don't Want to Be a Man*) (1918), Edgar Klitzsch's *Exzellenz Unterrock* (*Excellence Petty-Coat*) (1921), Paul Czinner's *Der Geiger von Florenz* (*Impetuous Youth*) (1926), his *Doña Juana* (1928) and Richard Eichberg's *Der Fürst von Pappenheim* (*The Masked Mannequin*) (1927). Reinhold Schünzel's cross-dressing comedy *Viktor und Viktoria* (*Viktor and Viktoria*) (1933) falls into the Nazi period but continues the theme of cross-dressing from the Weimar Period. This output of explicit and implicit representations of homosexuality has given the period a privileged status in the history gay and lesbian film, particularly in early works that established the field (see Dyer 1990; Weiss 1992; Russo 1995). The National Socialists censored films such as *Different from the Others* and *Girls in Uniform*, blacklisted directors, destroyed the gay movement's infrastructure and deported gays and lesbians to concentration camps. Queer films were destroyed or lost during World War Two and subsequently forgotten until the 1970s, when the gay and feminist movements rediscovered their significance (see, for example, Rich 1998a).

This chapter reads films that shaped the conventions for queer cinema, with particular emphasis on the two emblematic films of the Weimar Republic, *Different from the Others* and *Girls in Uniform*. The former created a blueprint for documentary realism that defines the gay activist documentary with equal-rights claims. The latter constitutes the foundational film of the genre of the all-female boarding school as the setting for lesbian desire. Other paradigmatic conventions were set in motion in Weimar Germany's productive film industry. Schünzel's *Viktor and Viktoria* exemplifies the trope of cross-dressing in a tension between narrative and camp, which enables pleasures of same-sex fantasies but narratively contains them in a happy ending of heterosexual couples. Pabst's *Pandora's Box* marks the lesbian character with cinematic codes and narrative strategies, reflecting the understanding of lesbian desire at that historical moment and shaping cinematic conventions and audience expectations for some time to come. Queer cinema, however, also extends to films that do not include characters that embody clearly circumscribed lesbian or gay identities. Thus, the chapter's final reading of Murnau's *Nosferatu* suggests the horror genre as an allegory for deviant desire.

The Activist Documentary

Oswald's *Different from the Others* provides a window into the relationship between community and medical discourse, film and social context, transgression and censorship in a complex, multi-layered plot. It humanises homosexuals to advocate for tolerance, offers a glimpse into the hidden subculture with footage from a masquerade ball, and attempts to incite an audience to mobilise against Paragraph 175. The film opens with the main character, the classical violinist Paul Körner, reading a newspaper about men of high standing who committed suicide. Kurt Sivers admires Paul's concert performance and takes violin lessons from him against his parents' will. When consulted, Magnus Hirschfeld explains to Kurt's parents that society's bigotry causes their son's suffering, not homosexuality.

Franz Bollek blackmails Paul after he has seen him with Kurt, but Paul refuses payment. Subsequently Franz breaks into Paul's home to steal money. Paul and Kurt return home unexpectedly and a fight ensues, during which Franz humiliates Kurt by suggesting that Paul pays him for his company. Unable to be consoled, Kurt leaves Paul. When Kurt's sister Else comforts Paul, he realises that she is in love with him but rejects her advances. Paul remembers his youth, and a flashback shows his affection for another male student at his boarding school and his visit to Hirschfeld who explained that homosexuals can make valuable contributions to humanity. Paul then recalls how he met Franz the first time at a gay masquerade ball. Franz is arrested for blackmail and charges Paul with Paragraph 175. The judge sentences Paul to one week in jail and Franz to three years, yet Paul is allowed to go home before beginning his sentence. He loses his contract with the concert agency and commits suicide. Hirschfeld consoles Kurt at Paul's deathbed by suggesting that he honour the memory of his friend and dedicate his life to changing prejudices.

The film's prolific director, Jewish pacifist Richard Oswald, was not a participant in the homosexual movement, but his insistence on his right to turn controversial and taboo topics into films made him a lightning rod for conservative attacks, often accompanied by anti-semitic screeds. These critical assaults against his films and person did not intimidate Oswald. In a statement in *Film-Kurier* in 1919 he claimed the right to address any topic of his choosing and threatened to sue anybody who would claim that he masked obscene films as educational (see Oswald 1990). Though he was at the height of his successful career in the 1920s, by the time he emigrated to Hollywood in 1938, he failed tragically (see Töteberg 1990: 113).

As the film's scientific-medical advisor, Hirschfeld, the openly gay director of the Institute for Sexual Science in Berlin and the founder of the SHC, strongly influenced *Different from the Others*. Hirschfeld continued the scholarship developed by turn-of-the-century sexologist and psychiatrist Richard von Krafft-Ebing who defined and catalogued sexual practices and identities, such as homosexual and heterosexual, masochistic and sadistic (see Krafft-Ebing 1965; Herzer 2001). A medical-scientific approach classified behaviour according to 'healthy' and 'pathological', overcoming a religious discourse, in which sexuality was supposed to serve procreation and homosexual acts were considered sinful (see Oosterhuis 2000; Mennel 2007). Hirschfeld committed his life to working for the acceptance of different kinds of sexual practices considered deviant, including homosexuality, transsexuality, cross-dressing, bisexuality and fetishism. He fought against Paragraph 175 – the criminalisation of the sex act between men – which had been part of the original German Criminal Law (1872), was intensified by the National Socialists, and remained law until 1994. In 1933 the National Socialists destroyed his Institute for Sexual Science and burned his books, whereupon Hirschfeld did not return to Germany from his last international speaking tour.

Different from the Others was highly controversial and at the centre of a scandal. Calls for censorship illustrate how homophobia was articulated through anti-semitism and vice versa (see Belach & Jacobsen 1990: 25). *Different from the Others* was banned in August of 1920 and could only be shown to doctors and educators (see Lamprecht 1968; Dyer 1990).

Numerous letters and reviews of the film appeared in *The Yearbook of Sexual Inbetweenness*, published by the SHC, covering a range of responses: some found the film's representation of homosexuality not subtle enough; other accused the film's audience of being 'of alien race', meaning Jewish (see Belach & Jacobsen 1990: 25–6, 29). One of the letter writers to *The Yearbook* associated homosexuality with Jewishness and expressed particular disgust with the dancing scene, in which men dressed up as women. Another letter writer called for censorship because educational films used shocking materials to make a profit, claiming that the film's demand for equal rights for gays constituted an outrage. The viewers who were critical of the film opposed cinema as a forum to discuss questions of homosexuality because film invites identification, which undermines objectivity and could seduce individual audience members to become gay. In contrast, another letter writer praised the film as tragic: 'Its effect was so impressive that the women around me – all belonging to the common people – cried' (cited in Belach & Jacobsen 1990: 32). The film thus empowered individual viewers, illustrated by one letter writer who announced that he was going to write a letter to his parents to reveal his gay identity.

The film also negotiates the divergent understandings of homosexuality at the time. The space of the bar, where Paul meets Franz, presents the subculture of the third sex, in which, according to film scholar Richard Dyer, gay men engaged in role-play between a younger type, called 'the *Bube* or *Bursch*, the large, handsome, open-faced working class lad', and the effeminate 'gay sub-cultural style, the *Tante* (literally, auntie)' (1990: 20, 19). Paul does not fully embody the role of the *Tante*, but his character includes accoutrements of femininity, such as an orientalist robe and a feminine posture. Dyer suggests that at the time Franz would have been recognised as a *Bube*, 'with broad, crude features' (1990: 20). It is Paul's downfall to enter the bar, the space of questionable characters, such as Franz.

Paul's relationship with Kurt, in contrast, follows the model of male homosexuality anchored in the Greek ideal of the pedagogical and platonic eros, which idealised the two complementary types of a boy 'poised on the brink of adolescence, and the older athlete', referenced by the statue in Paul's room (Dyer 1990: 23–4). This understanding of homosexuality characterises Paul's wholesome friendship at school and his love for Kurt. The passionate student/teacher relationship defines Paul and Kurt, and the film does not show them engaged in a sexual relationship. Squarely situated in the sphere of high culture, they do not venture into subcultural spaces together. The two relationships, of which each is associated with a different understanding of homosexuality, and a different setting, mark Paul as a dual character, a continuing code for homosexuals.

Actor Conrad Veidt, who plays Paul, at the time was 'a heart-throb, a popular pin-up in the film magazines' (Dyer 1990: 14), who in the same year played Cesare, a somnambulist with a secret double life, in the most famous German expressionist film *Das Cabinet des Dr. Caligari* (*The Cabinet of Dr. Caligari*) (1920). Veidt's roles informed his public persona and vice versa, typical for the star system that emerged in the Weimar Republic, when film stardom became a site to project and negotiate gender roles via the embodiment of the new man or the new woman, and emerging gay, lesbian and transsexual identities. In addition to Conrad Veidt, for example, famous female stars Asta Nielssen, Louise Brooks and Marlene Dietrich were linked erotically in public to men *and* women, got married *and* catered to same-sex audiences. The early star system, both in Weimar Germany and Hollywood, did not see sexual ambiguity as detrimental to star power (for a discussion of homosexuality in silent Hollywood, see Mann 2001). These early stars often portrayed transgressive gender roles as erotically attractive, as Marlene Dietrich famously did in Josef von Sternberg's *Der blaue Engel* (*The Blue Angel*) (1930). Continuing her performances in men's suits in her early films in Hollywood, *Morocco* (1930) and *Blonde Venus* (1932), both directed by von Sternberg, Dietrich embodies the erotic pleasure of cross-dressing and ambivalent sexuality on- and off-screen as part of her star persona that was exported to Hollywood.

Different from the Others, however, also relies on a set of technical and stylistic techniques to create a political aesthetic for the portrait of homosexuality. For example, scenes do not begin with establishing shots, the conventional overview of an environment to introduce viewers to the setting of action. Instead, *Different from the Others* repeatedly uses an iris, a round, moving mask that can open or close, to reveal more or less detail (see Bordwell & Thompson 2008). The iris opens from an individual character to locate his position in relation to his social setting. When Kurt and Paul play music together, the iris closes in on them, creating a moment of harmony but also entrapment. The narrative position of this particular shot signals the difference between the conventions of heterosexual and

Richard Oswald's *Different from the Others* (1919); Reinhold Schünzel as Franz (left) and Conrad Veidt as Paul

homosexual romance. In conventional love stories, the heterosexual couple coincides with the happy ending. In contrast, in films about gays and lesbians, up until the late 1970s, a homosexual union constitutes a problem for the narrative that has to be resolved by the film's conclusion, often tragically so.

Spatial compositions underscore social relations. The emphasis on background and foreground captures dynamic relationships between characters and their environments (see Steakley 2007). A shot in a bar situates Franz as part of the gay community but on its margins. At the ball masqueraded men and women are dancing in a polonaise, a subcultural tradition that encouraged social mixing (see Dobler 2003). Franz and Paul stand in front of the dancers, the former dressed in a white and the latter in a black costume. The colour contrast captures a trope for the representation of homosexuality by inscribing a polar difference, implying that the absence of heterosexuality produces a lack of differentiation.

A narrative frame integrates the melodramatic story in a public and political discourse. The film's ending returns to its opening of Paul studying a newspaper report about men who killed themselves, reading between the lines that they were homosexuals. The film's frame provides a socio-political context for Paul's individual fate and moves straight audience members from detached observers to informed readers. It instructs an audience about reading subtexts, a strategy employed by (sexual) minorities.

Yet, despite its political aim, the film ultimately privileges respectable 'male-identified gayness' (Dyer 1990: 27) in contrast to Hirschfeld's more radical and inclusive notions of homosexuality and sexual diversity. Given Hirschfeld's extensive participation in the film, we can assume that the valorisation of desexualised, masculine homosexuality in the private sphere and the marginalisation of the gay subculture was a conceit for the film's mainstream appeal in order to raise awareness about the negative effects of Paragraph 175.

Different from the Others shares with other progressive films of the era that it was made by a cast of writers, directors and actors, the majority of whom were persecuted by the National Socialists, left Germany, and either died shortly thereafter or lived abroad, often impoverished and forgotten, sometimes remaking themselves, as Veidt did, when he played Gestapo Major Strasser in Michael Curtiz's *Casablanca* (1942). The differences between *Different from the Others* and *Girls in Uniform*, however, illustrate the diversity of gay and lesbian cinema from its beginnings.

Lesbian Coming of Age

Leontine Sagan's successful feature-length narrative film *Girls in Uniform* appeared toward the end of the Weimar Republic in 1931, while the National Socialist Party was on the rise. Situated in a female boarding school espousing the discipline of Prussian militarism, the film portrays the forbidden desire between a teacher, Fräulein von Bernburg, and her fourteen-year-old student, Manuela. The school puts on Friedrich Schiller's drama 'Don Carlos' (1787–88) with Manuela playing the main role, a 'trouser's role' [*Hosenrolle*]. After the performance, the girls celebrate, and intoxicated Manuela publicly announces her love for Fräulein von Bernburg from the stage. In the midst of her passionate declaration, the headmistress walks in, is outraged, and has Manuela punished by isolating her in the sick ward. The treatment of Manuela leads to a confrontation between the head mistress and Fräulein von Bernburg. When Manuela then suddenly disappears the other girls frantically search for her, and find her walking

Leontine Sagan's *Girls in Uniform* (1931). Director Leontine Sagan and her actresses in uniforms

up the staircase to commit suicide by throwing herself from the banister. After they rescue her, Fräulein von Bernburg thanks the girls for preventing a disaster, and the headmistress leaves the scene in defeat.

Girls in Uniform is based on a play by Christa Winsloe from 1930 entitled *Gestern und Heute* (*Yesterday and Today*). After the film's success, Winsloe wrote the book *Girls in Uniform*, which was forbidden by the Nazi regime and published in Amsterdam and Vienna (see Winsloe 1983). She went into exile in France but later tried to return to Germany (see Schoppmann 1991). Toward the end of World War Two, she and her partner, Simone Gentet, were killed in France by men who claimed that Winsloe collaborated with the German occupation. After the war, a French trial against the murderers revealed that the accusation of Winsloe's collaboration was untenable (see Reinig 1983; Schoppmann 1991). The film's Austro-Hungarian director, Leontine Sagan, also emigrated, first to England, where she directed *Men of Tomorrow* (1932), and then to South Africa, where she worked in the theatre.

Academic discussions have focused on the film's politics in regard to the extent and limitation of its criticism of militarism and its portrayal of lesbianism (see Schlüpmann & Gramann 1981; Dyer 1990; von der Emde 1991; Rich 1998b). The foundational author of German film studies, Siegfried Kracauer, set the tone for the film's discussion in 1947. He praised *Girls in Uniform*, claiming that it was 'outstanding' in the manner in which it was 'candid in criticizing authoritarian behaviour', but in his final analysis he indicted the film because it did not advocate overthrowing the authoritarian system based on discipline but instead suggested 'its humanization', which ultimately 'would only be in the interest of its preservation' (1974: 226, 228–9). While B. Ruby Rich's influential essay from the late 1970s shifts the emphasis from the critique of authoritarianism to the film's lesbian subtext, she follows Kracauer's lead by arguing that Fräulein von Bernburg manipulates the girls 'to keep emotionalism in check and to make her charges more comfortable in their oppression' (1998b: 185).

Girls in Uniform integrates a feminist critique of patriarchy with a subtle portrait of lesbian desire. The film's account of the processes of interpellation into the military hierarchy, the role of eroticisation in this process and the limits of resistance illustrate French theorist Michel Foucault's argument that modern subjects internalise disciplinary power in such institutions as the boarding school, the jail and the insane asylum (see Foucault 1995). The film's spatial, temporal and aural organisation expresses the institutional repression determining the girls' lives. The film begins with an opening shot of heavy archways through which the girls march in rows and in step. The sound of a bell that structures their daily lives accompanies the *mise-en-scène* of Prussian neo-classical architecture and statues of kings and military heroes. Restrictions on communicating with parents, the prohibition on writing to each other and the limitation of books are intended to prevent individuation based on the assumption that reading induces fantasy and pleasure.

At the centre of the film's architectural composition are two staircases, one that symbolises the official flow of power in the institution, which is forbidden to the girls, and the other, where submerged desires and forbidden knowledges are transmitted, to which the girls have access. Gossip circulates on the latter staircase when Manuela initially meets girls who tell her about their collective crush on Fräulein von Bernburg. That staircase also becomes the stage for desire, when Manuela meets the admired teacher for the first time on the steps, which symbolise their power differential. Prior to this shot, close-ups of both of them, cross-cut with each other in the tradition of romantic films, anticipate their encounter. Its erotic appeal is not beyond the hierarchy of the institution but bound up in it.

Girls in Uniform locates a utopian moment within the militaristic disciplinary space in the collectivity of the students' female bodies when they are without their uniforms. When they prepare to go to bed, restrictions demand that their bodies are separated in wash cabins with curtains, but they open those, hold hands and embrace each other. One minor scene, played for comedic effect, encapsulates the subversive potential of the female body vis-à-vis the uniform. The rebel Ilse calls the other girls over to her and asks Marie, a chubby, naïve girl, to show the circle of girls around her what she is able to do. Marie takes a deep breath, expands her chest, and her breasts explode her uniform, so that buttons fly through the air. Ilse calls out to her laughing audience: 'That's a body, isn't it!?' Marie is embarrassed but proud. The physical body outdoes the disciplinary confinement of the uniform. The fact that the girls surround Marie and enjoy her voluptuous breasts creates an alternative to feminist film theorist Laura Mulvey's (1988a) argument that the female body functions as spectacle for a male audience.

In contrast to this collective utopian moment, the formation of individual desire does not take place outside of institutional structures. The girls are not only victims of the hierarchy but also positioned within it, being made to oversee each other and receiving swooning notes from younger students who are their female admirers. Desire for the teacher as an attempt at differentiation is bound to fail because she becomes an erotic object as a result of her position in the institution. The repetition of the desire for Fräulein von Bernburg is a case in point. When Manuela arrives, she receives a uniform with 'E.v.B.' [Elisabeth von Bernburg] stitched into it, a trace of the infatuation by the former wearer of the dress and her attempt to differentiate herself by inscribing individual desire into the uniform. Yet the uniform interpolates its wearers into the collective circulation of desire. After the play, Manuela dances with another girl who has taken the inscription of desire one step further by tattooing the initials 'E.v.B.' in her underarm. This challenges Manuela to declare her feelings for Fräulein von Bernburg publicly and claim that her object of affection reciprocates, since the beloved teacher has given her an intimate gift, a shirt. The teacher has transgressed the unwritten code of the institution that would allow erotic tension to be channeled by her, circulating in a delicate balance around her, while repressing her own desire.

Manuela and Fräulein von Bernburg's forbidden desire for each other drives the narrative forward. Manuela's love cannot be contained as infatuation, and the teacher implies reciprocity when she tells Manuela that expressing her feelings would make the other girls jealous. A kiss between them and Manuela's public declaration become two turning points in the narrative. The kiss takes place in the girls' communal dormitory and establishes Manuela's and Fräulein von Bernburg's passion for each other early in the narrative. After the teacher turns off the lights, all the girls kneel in their beds until she kisses each of them on the forehead. The camera moves from one girl to the next, each shot out of focus and bathed in soft lighting. Ilse subverts the sublime moment by whispering: 'Smooches with each one – wonderful!' She accords agency to Fräulein von Bernburg and enjoys her own voyeuristic pleasure in the homoerotic spectacle. The cinematic staging relies on romantic conventions of music when the soundtrack first creates suspense while Fräulein von Bernberg moves from bed to bed, and then rises to a crescendo while she kisses Manuela on the mouth who throws her arms passionately around her beloved teacher.

Audience members, however, can read *Girls in Uniform* as an explicit lesbian text or as a story of a girl who lost her mother and craves affection by a maternal substitute. Lesbian desire is located in the subtext, in superimpositions of shots of Fräulein von Bernburg and Manuela, and in the narrative structure around the kiss and the public declaration of a love that dare not speak its name. The play that the girls perform within the film, Schiller's 'Don Carlos', concerns forbidden love as a symbol of rebellion against repression. Quotations from the play take on a double-meaning in the context of the school, self-reflexively pointing to film's use of coded language. Gender is performed independent of biology, when the girls act in male and female roles. But individual lesbian desire is not imbued with revolutionary power or juxtaposed to the institution. The girls do not only swoon over Fräulein von Bernburg despite, but because of her authority. In the early twentieth century Sigmund Freud accorded the ability to fetishise only to men, a position that the film appropriates for girls in the role of desiring subjects (see Gamman & Makinen 1994). The film situates female fetishism of symbols of military power in a politically progressive narrative and ultimately captures the limitations of a politics based solely on desire.

This might, however, not have been the original intention of Christa Winsloe, whose book, written after the film, *Girls in Uniform*, departs in important ways from the film; for example, by coding individual girls, Mia and Oda, in addition to Manuela, explicitly as lesbians. The book extensively narrates Manuela's symbiotic relationship with her mother, locating the roots of Manuela's lesbian desire in her deep-seated love for her, which after her death extends to other feminine mothers. The film's rediscovery in the 1970s ignored the fusing of motherly and sexual love because the political understanding of lesbianism advocated equality and disavowed butch/femme and intergenerational relationships, which were seen as outdated and pre-feminist forms of lesbian identity that reproduced power differentials of man/woman, teacher/student and parent/child.

Manuela in Winsloe's literary description perceives herself as being in the wrong body, reminiscent of the turn-of-the-century understanding of inverts and the third sex. As a masculine woman, she is, however, not portrayed as 'mannish', the cultural image of the predatory lesbian constructed to denounce female same-sex attraction as deviant and denying femininity the ability to desire actively. In order to claim an explicit lesbian identity, Winsloe in her book version returned to an older understanding of sexual desire based on identification with the opposite gender. The film, to be palatable to a wide audience during the years that National Socialism was on the rise, erased the explicit coding of Fräulein von Bernburg, Manuela, and other characters as lesbians and created a subtext of submerged same-sex desire (on the production history of the film, see von der Emde 1991).

Cross-Dressing and Other Queer Allegories

Cross-dressing was a particularly popular trope associated with gender and sexuality in the films of the Weimar Republic, particularly in comedies. Films such as Lubitsch's *I Don't Want to Be a Man* and Eichberg's *The Masked Mannequin* included cross-gender performances. The many cross-dressing comedies in the Weimar Republic play to voyeuristic pleasure with sexual secrets and their revelations that surround the connection between gender and sexual desire. Schünzel, who played Franz Bollek in *Different from the Others*, employs cross-dressing in his film *Viktor and*

Viktoria to create gender confusion in a film that concludes with hetero-sexual couples. The musical *Viktor and Viktoria* follows the conventions of the romantic comedy of errors about two out-of-luck theatre actors, Viktor Hempel and Susanne Lohr, struggling to get roles. Susanne gets a part for Viktor who is sick and then continues impersonating him and becoming an international success as a man. Her cross-dressing motivates much confu-sion of gender and desire, until her true identity is revealed, and the film concludes by pairing Susanne and Viktor with appropriate heterosexual partners in the film's happy ending.

Appearing together in shots, the real and the false Viktor evoke the presence of two gay men. Film scholar Alice Kuzniar (2000) emphasises the aspect of fantasy when audience members can imagine a same-sex couple and suspend the knowledge of narrative truth, according to which, one of the characters belongs to the opposite sex. Cross-dressing chal-lenges the basic assumption that biological sex predetermines gender, which constitutes the basis of compulsory heterosexuality. In addition, female-to-male transvestism challenges patriarchal order. Susanne as Viktor performs in a sequence of challenges to prove her masculinity in male-bonding rituals: drinking whiskey, smoking a pipe, shooting a gun and defending her/himself against strong, jealous men. Narratives attempt to contain these moments of subversion initiated through cross-dressing. The happy ending (re)establishes the truth about gender and aligns two heterosexual couples with each other, retroactively giving permission to subversive fantasies, since they are marked as performance. Films such as *Viktor and Viktoria* negotiate between narrative containment and per-formative subversion that enable fantasies about alternative desires and identities.

These kinds of alternative desires were also embodied in gay and lesbian minor characters. Pabst's *Pandora's Box* includes one of the most famous iconic images of a lesbian character. The lesbian Countess Geschwitz appears in a minor role, one of the many characters seduced by the film's main character Lulu, played by Louise Brooks. The film is based on two turn-of-the-century plays by Frank Wedekind, *Erdgeist* (*Earth Spirit*) (1895) and *Die Büchse der Pandora* (*Pandora's Box*) (1904). Originally a dancer associated with the circus, promiscuous Lulu rises in society through marriage with a wealthy business man, Dr Ludwig Schön, but also falls into deep poverty when she flees to London after she is rescued by

G. W. Pabst's *Pandora's Box* (1929)

herfriends from the trial against her for his murder. She transgresses social norms, marked by her relationship with bourgeois Dr Schön, his son Alwa, and her flirtation with the lesbian Countess Geschwitz, whose presence highlights Lulu's transgressions. *Pandora's Box* codes Geschwitz as a lesbian in her first appearance through her masculine costume, her smoking and her active gaze at Lulu.

Lulu is characterised less by heterosexuality than by a transgressive sensuality that attracts members from different classes and genders. This makes her also an object of desire for lesbian viewers because she embodies the sexualised, self-confident, cosmopolitan New Woman who does not discriminate in her affection. It is that indiscriminate desire that brings about Lulu's downfall when she takes home Jack the Ripper in the film's final sequence who then kills her. Lulu's irreverence toward conventions leads to an iconographic lesbian scene in early cinema: Geschwitz attends Lulu's wedding with Dr Schön. Lulu and Geschwitz, dressed to complement and contrast each other, are staged in shot compositions so that their encounter becomes central to the scenes of the wedding party, decentring the highly symbolic heterosexual event. Geschwitz's blonde hair and black dress contrasts and compliments Lulu's black hair and white dress (similarly to the coding of Franz and Paul in *Different from the Others*).

Geschwitz does not interact with the other characters, standing alone at the wall, gazing only at Lulu, ignoring the events of the party. Later Lulu and Geschwitz dance closely together in eroticised movements in contrast to other couples around them whose dancing seems to be solely fulfilling social expectations.

The dance between Lulu and Geschwitz eroticises the possibility of lesbian desire beyond the film's narration, but Geschwitz alone carries no erotic appeal. Lulu (played by star Louise Brooks) remains the erotic focal point of the film, which also extends to her cross-dressing later in the narrative. Her group of friends, including Geschwitz, helps her escape from the trial for her husband's murder. On the ship to England, Lulu and her friends extort money from Geschwitz who thus becomes another victim of Lulu's seduction and betrayal. Left behind on the ship by Lulu and her group of admirers who flee on a boat, Geschwitz becomes a tragic figure, a role commonly accorded to lesbians for decades to come. In order to make it off the ship unrecognised, Lulu dresses as a working-class lad in pants and with a cap. Brooks' cross-dressing is part of the iconography of her as star (for stills of her as male vagabond in William A. Wellman's *Beggars of Life* (1928), see Weiss 1992: 25 and Brooks 2000: n.p.). In *Pandora's Box*, Lulu's cross-dressing occurs once she leaves Geschwitz behind, who does not reappear in the narrative. Geschwitz's gender transgression as a lesbian has been transferred and incorporated into the main character Lulu and continues in the extra-textual star persona of Louise Brooks.

The film's narrative marginalises the lesbian Geschwitz once she has served as a vehicle to enable the representation of Lulu's transgressive and seductive sexuality. *Pandora's Box* mobilises fantasies of lesbian desire through the dance between Geschwitz and Lulu but reduces the character of Geschwitz to frustrated longing, leaving her stranded on a ship with nowhere to go. The narrative, however, punishes both women for their transgressions; Geschwitz with loneliness and Lulu with violent murder.

While *Different from the Others*, *Girls in Uniform*, *Viktor and Viktoria* and *Pandora's Box* lay claim to filmic realism in the depiction of gays and lesbians, other films of the period create allegories of queer desire. Homosexuality's status as outside the norm and associated with subcultures leads to coded language, invisibility vis-à-vis dominant society and double lives. Thus, its cinematic expression often takes recourse to coded, metaphorical or allegorical representation, for example in the genre of the horror film. Murnau's *Nosferatu* famously embodies 'deviant' desire through a figure of horror, the vampire. Murnau himself, however, lived as an out gay man, first in Berlin and then in Hollywood (see Prinzler 2003; von Praunheim 2003).

Nosferatu opens in Bremen, Germany, where a happy couple, Hutter and his wife, live and work. Hutter travels to the Carpathian Mountains to sell a house in Bremen to Count Orlok. On his journey east, he stays at an inn where he reads about vampires. Once he crosses the bridge into the land of vampires, a mysterious coach drives him to a castle where doors open magically. The Count makes advances toward Hutter, especially after the guest has cut his finger, and Hutter later finds two marks on his neck. When the Count sees a picture of Hutter's wife, he admires her neck. Count Orlok then travels in a coffin via ship to Bremen, while Hutter rushes home as well. All the men on the ship die from the plague that travels with Orlok to Bremen. The Count moves into the house across the street from Hutter and his wife. The latter discovers that lying with a woman until the cock crows will destroy the vampire. She sacrifices herself to his prolonged bite, and the vampire disintegrates when the morning sun comes up.

Film scholar Harry Benshoff traces the development of the monster as a queer figure via the double life that characterises the vampire. While the monster opens up several avenues to read its symbolism, Benshoff emphasises the 'subtextual and connotative avenues' created by implicit and explicit prohibitions to portray homosexuality as a 'love that dare not speak its name', which thus becomes the 'shadowy Other' of 'normative heterosexuality' (1997: 14, 15). *Nosferatu*, as an expressionist film, is famous for its style. The Count, played by Max Schreck, appears sophisticated, slender and well-dressed with exaggerated long fingers, big ears and pale skin. Typical for expressionist film, *Nosferatu* emphasises shadows. In the film's most iconic scene, we only see the vampire's shadow on the wall, when he ascends the staircase to visit Hutter's wife.

In this film Nosferatu exudes an eroticism that is non-normative, non-procreative, bisexual and lethal. Typical for the horror film, the monster lives outside of social norms and kinship relations. His transience contrasts him to the rootedness of the Germans, localised in Bremen, and can also be read as an anti-semitic portrayal of Eastern European immigrants. To those who do not feel they have a place in wholesome heterosexuality, the film offers a belonging to an undefined queerness.

In conclusion, the films of the Weimar Republic set in motion the main conventions of queer cinema. While *Nosferatu* allows for a coded reading of queer desire, the explicit presence of the lesbian character Geschwitz in *Pandora's Box* illustrates a certain degree of normalcy, even if her desire remains tragically unfulfilled. *Viktor and Viktoria*'s cross-dressing enables subversive fantasies of alternative gender and desire, but their appropriation in a musical with narrative closure contains their subversive power.

The films discussed in this chapter reveal the diversity in the portraits of gender and desire in the Weimar Republic. Those who were politically active for gay rights used the new medium to solidify social identities and advocate for equal rights, including the articulation of a different desire. The crack-down of National Socialists attacked individual gays and lesbians, pushed the movement's infrastructure underground, violently destroyed archives and books of the sexologists, and forbad all explicit cinematic representation to homosexuality. Yet, below the ashes and the debris, the Weimar Republic remains as an exemplary period for the interface between politics and aesthetics that so defines queer cinema.

The two paradigmatic films *Different from the Others* and *Girls in Uniform* continue to influence gay and lesbian cinema. *Different from the Others* put in place the socially critical documentary, which still fulfills an important function as contemporary documentaries show. For example, Daniel Peddle's *The Aggressives* (2005) about butch black lesbians and Kirby Dick's *Outrage* (2009) about closeted right-wing politicians who support anti-gay legislation and politics in the US, continue that tradition. Similarly, the trope of the boarding school endures in films as a space where same-sex desire awakens and is negotiated through a nexus of power, from André Téchiné's *Les roseaux sauvages* (*Wild Reeds*) (1994) to Katherine Brooks' *Loving Annabelle* (2006). Even though, as the following chapters will show, the trajectory of queer cinema from its beginning in the Weimar Republic to films at the end of the twentieth and beginning of the twenty-first century does not follow a linear progression, these early films constitute important models for gay and lesbian films and evoke the central paradigms for queer film theory.

2   CAMP: WHERE TRASH MEETS ART

When in 1934 an agreement among the major studios in Hollywood to a system of self-censorship – the production code – went into effect, it formalised the verdict that homosexuality could not be represented in acts or words on the screen. Also named the Hays Code after its creator Will H. Hays, the production code was intended to uphold moral standards, and was most strictly enforced under helm of Joseph I. Breen from 1934 to 1954. Throughout the 1950s filmmakers began contesting it, so that it weakened during the 1960s and was abandoned in 1968. The production code circumscribed notions of decency and taste as heterosexuality without nudity, adultery, illicit sex, miscegenation and physical expression of passion, including kissing and sex acts.

The production code institutionalised the unspeakable nature of homosexuality in post-World War Two Hollywood films, which led to the formation of a queer aesthetic that was associated with subtexts, subversion and subcultures. Based on the prohibition to utter the words 'gay' or 'lesbian' on the mainstream screen, Hollywood films created narratives that circled around the impossibility to portray homosexuality explicitly. In contrast to the outspoken visibility of queers during the Weimar Republic, this interdiction of homosexuality in the Hollywood studio system produced queer aesthetic practices that included subversive strategies, such as camp and veiled subtexts, while the low-budget margins of the film industry embraced flamboyant sex and drag.

This chapter traces queer aesthetics across the boundaries of low and high art, small and big-budget, studio and independent production, genre and non-narrative films, and homophobic and homosexual politics in representative examples of American films from the late 1940s to the early 1970s. To set up the discussion about the emergence of queer film aesthetics, it begins with examples of Hollywood studio films with narratives that reflect the unspeakable nature of homosexuality. The discussion of three films in the chapter's first section, Alfred Hitchcock's *Rope* (1948), Joseph L. Mankiewicz's *Suddenly, Last Summer* (1959) and William Wyler's *The Children's Hour* (1961), illustrates how queerness created a narrative problem because it could not be made explicit, which in turn became a defining feature of Hollywood films about gays and lesbians until the 1970s. *Rope, Suddenly, Last Summer* and *The Children's Hour* portray the discursive effects of the prohibition to depict explicit homosexuality in the films' different degrees of homophobic stereotypes of murderous gays or self-hating lesbians. These big-budget and star-studded productions by major Hollywood studios created a discourse about gays and lesbians that relied on a dyad of homosexuality and homophobia.

The chapter's second section then moves on to capture camp as a defining feature of queer aesthetics. Cinematic camp has a special affinity to classic Hollywood of the 1940s and 1950s, when gays and lesbians worked in the studios under the explicit condition that their sexual identity was barred from filmic representation. The origins of camp, however, point beyond film, to earlier homosexual figures, such as the dandy, which emerged in eighteenth-century London and Paris and elevated aesthetics to a lifestyle, and aesthetic practices, such as orientalism, which embraced Far and Middle Eastern styles, endowed with erotic decadence and excess. Particularly the latter reappears in the spectacular wide-screen films and stars of classic Hollywood. Camp exaggerates roles in society through 'theatricality' and performs the artifice of gender with irony, undermining its presumed innate nature (see Babuscio 1999; Sontag 1999).

Camp connects Hollywood spectacles to experimental cinema, high art, trash cinema and popular culture through citation, appropriation, reception and recycling. Drag and camp quote the performance of stylised female Hollywood stars, recontextualising and recirculating their iconic images. For example, Maria Montez, who acted in the exotic locales and costumes of such orientalist melodramas, as Jon Hall's *Arabian Nights*

27

(1942) and Arthur Lubin's *Ali Baba and the Forty Thieves* (1944), became the model for the flamboyant drag performer Mario Montez, who worked with both underground filmmaker Jack Smith and Andy Warhol in the 1960s and 1970s.

Because camp cuts across experimental avant-garde film, popart and trash cinema, the chapter's second section connects analyses of individual films by directors Edward D. Wood Jr., Kenneth Anger, Jack Smith, Andy Warhol and John Waters to highlight their shared queer aesthetics. During the 1950s, Wood made B-movies, those low-budget features that filled the second half of the conventional double-bill film screenings with cheap genre films, such as horror, western and science fiction. Later, Wood also directed sexploitation, part of 'exploitation cinema', films that embodied 'tastelessness', yet were less defined by their content than by the ways in which it could be promoted to draw audiences (see Watson 1997: 78–80). Created for a distribution and exhibition circuit parallel to Hollywood's national theatre chains, B films featured 'forbidden images of nudity, drug addiction, childbirth, and venereal disease' (Heffernan 2004: 4; for an overview of the B-movie industry, see Schaefer 1999). Working on the margin of the studio system, however, allowed Wood to take on taboo topics and make his low-budget film about transsexualism, *Glen or Glenda* (1953), which this chapter discusses as foundational for queer aesthetic, even if unintentionally so.

Kenneth Anger, Jack Smith and Andy Warhol, in contrast, are associated with the experimental avant-garde, defined by its 'willfully nonconformist' attitude, often exploring the 'possibilities of the medium itself' (Bordwell & Thompson 2008: 355). Warhol reached global fame as representative of popart, the 1960s art movement that integrated mass-produced popular culture and advertisement into fine arts, whereas Anger and Smith received limited exposure beyond cinephiles of the avant-garde, film historians and lovers of experimental queer cinema, even though they influenced other important directors. The works of these three filmmakers, however, share their access of queer subculture in forms of drag and camp, as do contemporary filmmaker John Waters' films. Waters began making films with shock value in the 1960s in Baltimore, a city defined by urban grittiness, B-movie houses and working-class culture that consciously positioned itself against Hollywood's home of the studio system, and New York's claim to avant-garde art. These films, though by very different directors, lack continuity editing, have highly artificial sets, and rely on anti-realist acting, which turns them into artifice and camp, in some instances intentional, in other instances an unintended result of the lack of a sufficient budget.

Whereas camp was more centrally associated with gay men and able to move into high art, lesbians were more commonly aligned with literary pulp and filmic sexploitation, the topic of this chapter's third and last section. Lesbians on screen thus tended to remain in the nether spheres of sexualised melodrama without access to the cosmopolitan realm of high art. Sexploitation films, a result of the weakened production code, regularly portrayed sexualised lesbians, such as the predatory butch and the sexy but child-like femme. Joseph P. Mawra's *Chained Girls* (1965), for example, discussed in this chapter's last section, creates a voyeuristic gaze at 'deviant desire'. As another consequence of the weakening of the production code, however, the difference between mainstream studio films and B movies became less defined, which this chapter illustrates with the reading of Radley Metzger's *Therese and Isabelle* (1968) and Robert Aldrich's *The Killing of Sister George* (1968), two lesbian films. They serve as examples of relatively high-budget films that reveal certain aspects of lesbian life, for example, butch/femme relationships and bar culture, but create a titillating voyeuristic gaze, transforming the lesbian characters into spectacles of deviance. The presence of the figure of the lesbian in the 1960s thus went hand in glove with a blurring of the boundaries between trash, the low-budget 'bad' films and the widely distributed mainstream.

While a reading of lesbian pulp and sexploitation as camp forms the basis of their contemporary cult following, this was not their original mode of address or reception. Until the second wave women's movement, which triggered a radical shift in thinking about gender and sexuality, the filmic representation of lesbian sex carried with it the connotation of exhibitionism for straight male voyeurism, no matter how artistic the director, sophisticated the literary basis or prominent its actors. These kinds of erotic images of lesbians on the margin of the mainstream are, however, connected to camp through their hyperbolic embrace of artifice and deviance. The outrageously trashy sexualised lesbians in sexploitation are linked to their Hollywood counterparts – those self-hating suicidal victims of their own monstrous desires that they cannot control – as their inverted mirror image. Those images silenced in mainstream film in the name of good taste and normal values during the height of the production code,

29

reappeared in trash cinema as a boisterous in-your-face badness with increasing force until the explosion of the gay rights movement in the late 1960s.

Hollywood's Homophobia/Homosexuality

Hollywood's production code explicitly forbad the depiction of explicit or inferred sex acts or perversion, which necessitated a veiled language to express sexual desire and activity (for the full text of the production code, see Belton 1996). Paradoxically, because homosexuality could not be mentioned on screen, its unspeakable nature, in turn, mobilised narratives which made homosexuality readable through its effects. In the three films discussed in this opening section, the fact that homosexuality constituted a secret, shapes the plot.

Hitchcock's *Rope* serves as a brief introduction to this particular structure, typical of Hollywood's treatment of homosexuality under the production code. In the film, two men, Brandon and Philip, live together in a New York apartment. They have killed their fellow student David and hidden his corpse in a chest. They throw a party, attended by David's father, aunt and fiancée Janet, his good friend Kenneth, who is Janet's former boyfriend, and Rupert, who was the teacher of all four young men. Rupert had influenced Brandon with his philosophy of intellectual superiority. During the party Rupert becomes increasingly suspicious and finally deduces that Brandon and Philip have killed David. The action takes place entirely in the space of the apartment with fluid camera movements and no cuts. Repeatedly the composition of the *mise-en-scène* positions the chest with the dead body in the centre of the shot. In one long shot, the camera focuses on the chest with the secret, while the party conversation continues off-screen. *Rope* is loosely based on the case of Nathan Leopold and Richard Loeb, who famously engaged in a thrill kill in 1924 in Chicago of a young boy and were known to be gay lovers (about the case, see Higdon 1999).

Even though neither the two main characters, nor any other figure in the story, are explicitly identified as gay in the film, their homosexuality seems to be a self-understood fact. French filmmaker François Truffaut, for example, summarises the film's premise: 'Two young homosexuals strangle a school friend just for the thrill of it' (1985: 179). How can the homosexuality of these murderous characters be so self-evident if 'gay' is never uttered in the film? Is the fact that two men live together enough to raise suspicion? Are Brandon and Philip too close for being 'just friends'? Or does the unspeakable deed of murder stand in for acts that are even more horrific and unmentionable? Is there something queer about them?

The murder binds Brandon and Philip to each other and metonymically functions for unspeakable gay sex. *Rope* opens with a medium close-up of the act of murder, which positions David between Brandon and Philip being strangled by both of them. Once David is dead, Brandon and Philip engage in a conversation that could also be post-coital: 'How did you feel?' one asks the other, 'When?' to which the other one responds, 'During it.' 'When he went limp, I was exhilarated.' They argue whether they should turn the lights on or off and confirm to each other that they could not have done it with the lights on. Philip, the artistic one, often a code for gay, becomes increasingly hysterical, and thus feminised. Brandon uses 'we' when he refers to both of them, as when he suggests 'We deserve a real holiday', as if they constitute a couple and not roommates with separate lives.

The character composition in the film repeats mirroring triangles. David is the conduit between Brandon and Philip. Rupert also refers to Brandon being busy 'trying to organise the other two points of the triangle', which refers to David, his best friend Ken and his girlfriend Janet. In the latter triangle, the two men exchanged Janet, paralleling the exchange of David between Brandon and Philip. Thus, the gay triangle relies on murder, whereas the heterosexual triangle implies sex. The last triangle consists of Brandon, Philip and Rupert, when Rupert returns to the apartment later that evening, and the three of them are repeatedly arranged in triangular compositions on the screen. Even though Rupert functions as the detective, the film hints that he might be of the same persuasion: single, surrounded only by boys, called 'peculiar' by the maid who is obviously fond of him, to which he, however, is oblivious.

The secret of homosexuality reflects larger societal structures. Scholar of Queer Film Studies, D. A. Miller suggests that the force of the production code functioned in a larger societal context that tolerated homosexuality when it was 'kept out of sight'; consequently gayness relied on 'connotation' (Miller 1991: 123). The dead invisible body at the centre of the film's spatial and visual composition that centrally organises the narrative, functions like homosexuality. *Rope* stages the problem of homosexuality by hiding what is in plain sight, but also by creating a dialogue that takes on new meaning, if we presume the characters are gay. The film's double talk mimics the coded language of gay men at the time. *Rope* discredits homosexuality by connecting it to violent death, an association that is common in films that employ a homophobic subtext for spectatorial pleasure.

The link of male homosexuality and death, parallel to femininity and hysteria, also centrally organises Mankiewicz's *Suddenly, Last Summer*, which mobilises gay stereotypes but also invites a reading of camp. Based on a play by the celebrated gay playwright Tennessee Williams, *Suddenly, Last Summer* tells the story of Sebastian, the son of rich and overbearing widow Violet Venable (Katherine Hepburn), who died while vacationing in Spain with his cousin Catherine (Elizabeth Taylor). Since then, Catherine has been institutionalised in a mental asylum. It becomes increasingly apparent that Violet wants famous psychiatrist Dr Cukrowicz to perform a lobotomy on Catherine to prevent her from telling the story of her son's death. Dr Cukrowicz helps Catherine remember and recount her repressed memories, which include a rape by a married man after a Mardi Gras ball a year prior. At the film's conclusion, Dr Cukrowicz induces Catherine's account about the traumatic incidents of the past summer in Spain. Sebastian had pulled her into the water at a beach, exposing her in a wet see-through bathing suit to young Spanish men looking at her through a fence that segregated tourists from the poor people at the free beach. Later, a mob of those poor, young men followed Sebastian who tried to escape by walking up a hill, surrounded him, and finally killed him by devouring his body.

The film rearticulates homosexual codes in homophobic terms. *Suddenly, Last Summer*'s absent main character, Sebastian, is marked as gay, without this ever being said, by his heightened sense of aesthetics that the film discredits as unproductive, since he writes only one poem per year. The perception of his gayness also relies on psychoanalytic models that suggest that homosexuality results from a symbiotic relationship between sons and their mothers. As in *Rope*, homosexuality has to be read by its effects. Catherine reveals that Sebastian used first his mother and then her to procure men for him. Femininity becomes a mask for gay men that denies women independent agency. Miller suggests that Catherine is a 'device for giving utterance to the story of Sebastian, the homosexual', because he cannot appear as an embodied figure in the film (Miller 1999:

97). To make the case in point, the camera never shows Sebastian's face, even in the scenes that represent Catherine's memory of his death. The film associates homosexuality with upper-class men and projects primitivism onto the Mediterranean Other that consumes Sebastian in a visceral response to his whetting their sexual appetite. Similar to the murder in *Rope*, cannibalistic murder 'figures gay sex', connecting unspeakable homosexuality with violence and destruction (Ohi 2001: 268).

Despite this denunciatory employment of homophobic codes, the film creates such artifice through the flamboyant acting and decadent setting that it simultaneously invites a reading of camp. Violet Venable arrives in her entry hall to greet her guests in an elevator, while reciting quotations from her dead son. The setting of Sebastian's garden, with flesh-eating plants and excessive vegetation, shows denaturalised nature as artifice. Hollywood could not portray homosexuality without homophobia, but could also not engage in homophobic discourse without acknowledging traces of homosexuality, creating the dyad of homosexuality and homophobia.

Two years later, also based on a play, Wyler's *The Children's Hour* centres on the unspeakable nature of lesbian desire and the discursive effects it produces. Like *Suddenly, Last Summer*, *The Children's Hour* includes famous Hollywood stars, Shirley MacLaine, Audrey Hepburn and James Garner. Based on a 1934 play by Lillian Hellman of the same title, which, in turn, fictionalised a case that took place in 1810 in Edinburgh, Scotland, *The Children's Hour* tells the horrific consequences of a homophobic witch-hunt in a tight-knit community (on the historical case, see Faderman 1994). Hinging on the prohibition to speak the term 'lesbian' publicly, the secret is constitutive of the film's narrative development.

Karen Wright and Martha Dobie run a small all-girls school. Martha's Aunt Lily, a former Broadway star, works as an elocution instructor at their school, but Martha kicks her out because she accuses Martha's relationship to Karen to be pathologically close. Karen is engaged to Joe Cardin, the local doctor and nephew of Mrs Amelia Tilford, the rich woman of the small town. Mary Tilford, one of the girls in the school, granddaughter of Mrs Tilford, feigns illness and when her grandmother picks her up from school, Mary whispers a secret into her ear and never has to return to the school. Subsequently, the other parents take their children out of school. When it turns out that Mary denounced Martha and Karen as lesbians, they sue, but lose because Aunt Lily does not appear in court to support their

William Wyler's *The Children's Hour* (1961)

case. Joe, Karen and Martha become increasingly isolated from the rest of the community, and the suspicion among the three finally tears them apart. Karen accuses Joe of not trusting her and Martha doubts her own motivation in her relationship to Karen, wondering whether in fact, she loves Karen. Joe's aunt reappears at the school to apologise since Mary has confessed to lying, but the two women's social lives and relationships have been destroyed. While Karen goes for a walk, Martha hangs herself. The film ends with Martha's funeral, at which Karen walks away from everybody, including Joe.

William Wyler had turned Hellman's play into a film once before, in 1936, with the title *These Three*, also based on a script written by Hellman and also produced by the studio of Samuel Goldwyn. In 1936 the production code was in full force, and thus Hellman emptied the script out of any lesbianism. Instead, Mary accuses Martha of having an affair with Joe. In addition, as scholar of queer film Patricia White points out, 'Martha is demasculinized' from her character description in Hellman's original play (1999: 26). Most importantly, however, the rescripting of the plot allows for a happy ending, in which Martha finds out the truth, confronts Mary Tilford and her grandmother, and enables the reunion of Joe and Karen in Austria. White explains: 'The very fact that *These Three*'s Martha doesn't have to die shows how gratuitous and calculated queer movie deaths are (the Code requires that crime and vice must be paid for). ... Having the lesbian pass for straight in this film saves her life' (1999: 27).

The later film version, *The Children's Hour*, offers a sensitive portrait of the relationship between the two female main characters, focusing on the negotiation of their intimacy. Yet the film casts Karen in a decidedly more positive light than Martha, whose motivations invite doubt from the outset. Karen cares for her friend Martha and the children, and loves Joe, planning a baby and marriage. By situating her in a heterosexual relationship, the film constructs the nature of her relationship to the children and Martha as intimate care but devoid of any sexual desire. In contrast, because Martha is single, her desires are less clearly defined. She pays excessive attention to Karen, and is dependent on her from the outset. Her moodiness and unfriendliness to Joe, viewers can infer, reflect jealousy and envy of his masculinity. Martha has no associations with men and surrounds herself only with women and girls. The film implies that Martha kicks out her aunt because she observed her intimate desire for Karen. Whereas Karen looks to a bright future with Joe, Martha melancholically remembers her past in college with Karen, embodying the lesbian's tragic and unfulfilled longing for the desirable, but unavailable, straight woman.

At the heart of the film lies the secret that Mary whispers into her grandmother's ear, reproducing the dynamic that surrounds homosexuality because the damage unravels from what cannot be heard by the audience. This silence contrasts with Aunt Lily's incessant talk about Martha's 'insane devotion' to Karen, who finally articulates the charge 'that Martha and I have been lovers'. Karen blames Mary in front of her grandmother: 'She is a bad girl – your Mary. She always has been. Wicked very young, wicked very old.' Mary's innately wicked nature enables her to perceive Martha's deviance before Martha herself does. White argues similarly about Mary's role in *These Three*, in which her sadism is more pronounced, 'this unnatural child is the relay of the film's unmentionable source material' (1999: 26).

The film fails to criticise the power of defamatory lies convincingly, since ultimately those lead Martha to suspect her lesbian identity. Once accused, Martha goes through a negative process of self-recognition: 'Every word has a new meaning ... friend ... woman.' Martha wonders: 'Maybe I love you the way they say I do ... I never knew what it was until they said it ... I'm guilty ... I never felt about anybody like I felt about you ... She found a lie with an ounce of truth ... I feel so damn sick and dirty...' The film condemns lies but then offers viewers the tragic self-realisation of the queer subject who articulates disgust at herself, thus authenticating the rumors as truth. *The Children's Hour* leaves the audience with Martha's suicide and Karen's loneliness. The ambivalent liberal discourse accuses the mean-spirited rumours around the two women, while validating its truth that tragically leads to Martha's death at her own hand.

Drag and Camp in Trash and Art

Queer aesthetics links trash cinema and B movies to experimental films and high art. A range of filmmakers, such as Edward D. Wood Jr., Kenneth Anger, Jack Smith, Andy Warhol and John Waters created a queer aesthetic by embracing the abject and perversions in the form of trash, drag and camp. Wood continued the Weimar Republic tradition of horror films with queer subtexts when he made films on the margin of Hollywood, the B film industry, during the 1950s. Unable to partake in the Hollywood studio system, he instead created films with low budgets that relied on bad acting, non-continuous editing, cheap settings and costumes and non-coherent narratives. His films use genres, such as horror or science fiction, to tell stories about transsexuals, vampires or aliens, including *Bride of the Monster* (1955), *Plan 9 from Outer Space* (1959), *Night of the Ghouls* (1959) and, later in the 1970s, low-budget adult and sexploitation films such as *'Necromania': A Tale of Weird Love!* (1971). Born in 1924, he became increasingly depressed and alcoholic, and died indigent and homeless in 1978. Wood identified as a straight man who liked to wear women's clothes with a particular fetish for angora sweaters (see Grey 1992). He loved early horror films, such as Tod Browning's *Dracula* (1931), starring Bela Lugosi, which continued the homoerotic and expressionist traditions from the Weimar Republic in the B-movie category, brought to the US by exile directors from Germany, such as Edgar G. Ulmer (see Isenberg 2004).

Wood's *Glen or Glenda* exemplifies camp created on the margins of Hollywood. It addresses cross-dressing simultaneously in a fictional and a documentary format mixed with aspects of the horror film in different narrative strands. The film opens with a suicide of a man wearing women's clothes. A detective then visits a psychologist who explains cross-dressing with two examples: one, the story of cross-dresser Glen who falls in love with Barbara, which enables him to overcome his transvestism; and two, the story of Allan, a pseudo-hermaphrodite (somebody with external genitalia of one sex and internal sex organs of another) who decides to undergo sex-reassignment surgery and become a woman. The film repeatedly returns to the dialogue between the psychiatrist and the inspector, in which the former explains these two cases to the latter. The narrative is intercut with scenes of Bela Lugosi, iconic actor of early horror films, surrounded by books, skeletons and laboratory items, sitting in an armchair making pronouncements with imposing intonation in his Eastern European accent, while suspenseful music plays and the wind howls. The horror film conventions continue in the educational narrative, for example, when Glen's mother screams in terror upon seeing Glen in women's clothes. By integrating aspects of the horror film with a narrative about sexual deviance, *Glen or Glenda* points to the horror genre's cinematic language as a sign system for sexual otherness.

One central sequence in this film lacks any *mise-en-scène*, continuity or claims to realism, and gives over the action entirely to the sphere of the symbolic and the performative, possibly intended as a nightmare or dream sequence. Characters of the narrative appear, such as Barbara, Glen and Lugosi, but also new characters who fulfill a symbolic function, such as the devil, a priest, a chorus and children. First Barbara, then Glen as Glenda, appear in front of an entirely black backdrop. After an apparent explosion, Barbara is caught underneath a log, which Glen lifts up. Towards the end of the sequence, Barbara and Glen appear dressed in the same clothes. Scenes of Lugosi are intercut, in which he recites lines from the famous nursery rhyme: 'What are little boys made of?/Frogs and snails and puppy-dogs' tales/What are little girls made of?/Sugar and spice and all that's nice', which is later repeated by children. At a later point, Lugosi declares: 'Beware, beware of the big green dragon that sits on your doorstep.'

Several other scenes stage erotic compositions with sado-masochistic overtones accompanied by jazz and tango on the soundtrack, including a man whipping a woman lying on a sofa, and a woman lounging seductively on the sofa, tearing off her clothes and grinding her body. Scenes emphasise the act of looking: for example, a woman looking at herself in a mirror, or Glen watching one of these staged scenes. A group of people point their fingers at Glen, and hands appear on the screen, until they overpower Glen, and we see his hand reaching out from the crowd. Intercut are images of the city, of a baby screaming, and of running buffalo. The sequence ends with Glen and Barbara sitting together. Glen tells her about his cross-dressing and she accepts him.

The film remains ambivalent about how an audience is supposed to read the sequence – an externalisation of an inner conflict, a dream, a nightmare or a symbolic acting out of the social structure surrounding the isolated gender non-conformist? Reminiscent of expressionism, the sequence reduces narrative conflict to symbolic action, such as pointing at the outsider and cornering him. The repetition of the rhymes emphasises the socialisation process of children into gendered beings. Female bodies act out of desire and seductive femininity. The lack of narrative and continuity editing prevents an audience from identifying with Glen, the typical liberal Hollywood formula of inviting understanding for those who are different. Instead, the film self-confidently takes the point of view of sexual deviance, while accusing the processes of normalising gender through looks, socialisation and discursive strategies. The reduction from narrative to symbolic acts paradoxically results from the film's low budget that prevents a realist setting and acting, and continuity editing, both of which are preconditions for the suspension of disbelief and identification. *Glen or Glenda* approximates expressionist and experimental cinema with a particular emphasis on the performativity of gender. Wood's own invisible difference – supposedly he wore women's lingerie while serving as a Marine in World War Two – might have made him sensitive to those film traditions that continued queer subtexts, such as the expressionist horror film (Grey 1992: 20). *Glen or Glenda* develops a cinematic language to address perverse desires, not despite its low budget but because of it.

Kenneth Anger's films also create a cinematic language for queer aesthetics with a low budget but belong to the realm of experimental and avant-garde cinema, which garners the respect of critics in the established art and film world for its artistic, intellectual and political dimensions. Anger worked as an experimental filmmaker and created an eclectic mix of films that do not clearly belong to one film movement or category but constitute important examples of queer aesthetics before the emergence of the modern gay rights movement.

Anger's short film *Kustom Kar Kommandos* (1965) brilliantly creates camp without narrative through the simple action of a young man stroking his custom-built car with a giant powder puff. The film rewrites masculinity by unearthing the car's fetishistic quality and eroticising the relationship between the young man and his automobile. The scene relies on extreme colouring, bathing the entire scene in saturated colours of pink, light blue and extreme red of the lip-like car seats, feminising the setting. The pop ballad 'Dream Lover' accompanies the visuals. The staging turns the everyday, working-class hobby into artifice. Camp ironises the masculine hobby through the use of the powder puff and the 'feminine' colours. The incongruity of the masculine sphere of the garage with the fetish of the machine and the feminine sphere evoked by the powder puff transports the everyday object and activity into a dreamlike state of camp. The absence of narrative intensifies the colour, setting and music to create the essence of camp. *Kustom Kar Kommando* has buried in its title the abbreviation KKK, a reference to one of the most heinous political groups that employs fetishism. As typical for camp, Anger subverts the racist fetishisation of Aryan hetero-masculinity but does not take an explicit political stance. The ambivalence that results from camp's openness to interpretation and the subtlety of its intervention constitutes its political productivity but also its limitation.

Anger's *Scorpio Rising* (1964) similarly finds and cinematically recreates camp out of ethnic and working-class masculinity of young Italian-Americans bikers in the 1960s. The film reproduces men's fetishisation of their bikes with close-ups of isolated parts that are carefully lit. It stages individual men who adorn themselves with jeans, leather and silver chains, standing and reclining in poses in different stages of dress and undress. The compositions position individual men surrounded by photos of icons of masculine outlaws, such as James Dean and Marlon Brando. At a Halloween party, the men engage in homosocial erotic games and faux violence in the form of sexualised initiation rites. The ambivalence of camp, however, also leaves open how we are to read the Nazi flags in the setting's background: as icons for a pose of an oppositional stance, as political statements, or as undermining the latter through the film's recontextualization. The film celebrates a masculine world and positions these men as its sexual spectacle, which is the locus of the film's ironic incongruence of machismo culture and feminising objectification that turns the ethnographic filmmaking of the 1960s working-class culture into camp.

Jack Smith shares with Wood and Anger that he produced camp by embracing trash and recycling Hollywood stars and aesthetics in low-budget film. Smith was an experimental filmmaker, associated with the underground art scene in New York during the 1960s, who understood his work more explicitly as political than Wood and Anger saw their films. Like Wood, he was poor throughout his career, unable to make a profit from his artistic work, and died of AIDS in 1989. Smith also shared with Wood the influence of filmic fantasies of alternative worlds during his youth when he identified with 1940s Hollywood star Maria Montez. His filmic aesthetics exaggerate the already hyperbolic performance of Hollywood feminine beauty and exotic and arabesque settings through 'flaming', while endowing his films and later performances with a political rage against sexual repression. Smith's filmic aesthetics continues the orientalism of Weimar Cinema, associated with homosexuality (for example, in *Different from the Others*) and the Baroque as an expressive style of hyperbole. After his controversial film *Flaming Creatures* (1963) was censored over its explicit nudity, Smith felt betrayed by archivists and distributors (see Mary Jordan's film documentary *Jack Smith and the Destruction of Atlantis*, 2006). Subsequently, he began screening his films himself, editing them in the process, so that each film only existed in the moment of its projection. The camp that pervades his films cites classic Hollywood at its height, appropriating the exaggerated performance of femininity in orientalist settings for a mythical discourse of (homo)sexual liberation.

Smith and pop artist Andy Warhol overlapped and collaborated but only Warhol achieved international renown as the iconic artist of popart, while Smith died poor and mostly forgotten. Like Wood, Anger and Waters, Warhol surrounded himself with a group of queers, cross-dressers and artists. Warhol, of course, is not primarily known as a film director. A small collection of Warhol's long-term project *Screen Tests* is available on DVD, and they illustrate the formalism of the project, which pares down camp from excess to its minimalist essence. Between 1964 and 1966, Warhol filmed visitors to his studio, called 'The Factory', whom he believed to have star quality, each in a four-minute screen test and carrying the first name of its individual subject as its title. Warhol collected more than five hundred of these *Screen Tests* in several compilations. His *Screen Tests* (1964–66) illustrate queer aesthetics based on the refusal of narrative and *mise-en-scène* and in the absence of gay or lesbian identity.

Warhol's *Screen Tests* are part of a larger project that turns the banal into high art, creating beauty out of the everyday. *Susan* shows Susan Bottomly with dramatic lighting that makes one half of her face appear glamorous; the lack of narrative invokes fantasies. In *Dennis*, the posture and positions of filmmaker and actor Dennis Hopper invite projections of emotions. Without an explicitly queer content, the straight-on shot gives over these faces to the realm of aesthetics but emphasises surface instead of depth. The different *Screen Tests* produce a hypnotic effect when characters, such as Nico or Freddy Herko, move around within and out of the frame. When images are out of focus, as in *Richard*, they evoke cinematic traditions of faded memories. Characters embody the 1960s cool, such as when Lou Reed in *Lou* appears in his sunglasses, drinking coca cola. Jane Holzer in *Jane* brushes her teeth, in an extreme close up, contrasting glamour with the mundane, transforming the latter into an erotic activity. The *Screen Tests* employ the mechanics of cinema that create mystery, such as lighting, or invite projection, such as soft focus, creating artifice with a minimalist and formalist approach.

While Warhol incorporated trash into high art and the cosmopolitan world of New York, Waters brought melodrama, performance art and street theatre into low-budget films that are intentionally shocking, campy, trashy, disgusting, entertaining, hilarious and self-confidently set in working-class Baltimore. Waters, who began making films in the early 1960s, continues to make films, carefully negotiating his former place on the margin of acceptable taste with the mainstreaming forces of the culture industry. For example, his early film *Hairspray* (1988) was remade in 2007 by mainstream film director Adam Schankman with Hollywood stars John Travolta, Michelle Pfeiffer, Christopher Walken, Queen Latifah and Jerry Stiller and also became a hit on Broadway as a musical. Since the early 1960s, Waters has made over twenty films, and by the 1990s, he increasingly left behind the shock value of his earlier films. But he still situates himself self-consciously in a tradition of camp, answering to Hollywood from the margin. For example, his film *Cecil B. Demented* (2000) connects an anarchic plot with a homage to filmmaker Cecil B. DeMille, director of flamboyant Hollywood studio films *Cleopatra* (1934) and *The Ten Commandments* (1956).

The exploitation of scandals, taboos, shock, disgust and bad taste on day-time television and reality shows has normalised the formerly subversive aspects of Waters' anti-bourgeois cinematic strategies. Subsequently, he embraced more conventional narrative film and situated his films in suburbia, for example his *Serial Mom* (1994). He appeared as 'John' on the American cartoon series *The Simpsons* in a 1997 episode, entitled 'Homer's Phobia', in which the father, Homer Simpson, is afraid that his son, Bart, might turn gay. The episode used trashy objects to negotiate how they can simultaneously reflect Homer's working-class bad taste and be revalorised by John's aesthetic camp sensibilities. The joke pivots on Homer's excitement about the valorisation of his trash until he understands that this would associate him with homosexuality. The episode earned awards for outstanding anti-homophobic television programming and marked the entrance of marginal queer cultural production into television, popular culture and its vernacular.

However, two decades earlier, the American cultural landscape looked quite different, and Waters' film *Desperate Living* (1977) includes a range of perverse sexual behaviours, fetishes, life-styles and identities culled from exploitation cinema, pulp and sexual underground culture that could not circulate in the mainstream. *Desperate Living* illustrates the connection between trash, low-budget and experimental art-house cinema. In the film, suburban hysterical housewife, Peggy Gravel, kills her husband with the help of her heavy-set black maid Griselda. They then run from the law, embodied by a cop with an underwear fetish, and finally Peggy and Griselda become lovers in a makeshift town of queers called Mortville ruled by Queen Carlotta who is surrounded by an army of sexy leather-men. Peggy and Grizelda stay with the lesbian couple Muffy St. Jacques and Mole McHenry, and Peggy rises in the hierarchy of the faux medieval town.

The opening of *Desperate Living* in the upper-class suburban home of the Gravel family cites the convention of the melodrama with Mrs Gravel exaggerating her performance of a nervous breakdown. The sexual relationship between Peggy and Griselda unearths the homoerotic tension in the melodramatic interracial relationships between female characters in the classic Hollywood women's films, such as Douglas Sirk's *Imitation of Life* (1959). The actors self-confidently perform with an obvious lack of professional training. The set of the medieval town of perverts, Mortville, was made 'almost entirely out of garbage' (Waters 1995: 167), literalising the association of queers with trash on the margin of society. Waters also recycles, and in that process, resignifies and revalorises trash film culture, such as the continuum of porn, softcore, sexploitation and fetish culture. Muffy, played by the stripper Liz Renay, consistently wears sexy outfits, as if in a porn film. Mole and Muffy perform their butch and femme roles in exaggerated ways, pointing to the absurdity of the hypersexalisaton of exploitation film while valorising its blunt and unapologetic address of voyeurism.

The recontextualisation of fetish culture, however, ironises and thus undermines the power of the fetish. Peggy and Grizelda as lovers create an incongruous contrast of the interracial, interclass sexual relationship, citing the fetish of the big black and dominant woman associated with lower-class culture. Fetish culture, a socio-sexual system organised around a fetish that traditionally stands in for sexual intercourse and functions for sexual arousal, such as high heels, leather, whips, latex or big breasts, often connote power differentials. The film refers to gay underground sex culture with the presence of in a group of leather-men that form the Queen's army, one of whom repeatedly strips for the fairy-tale dominatrix of Mortville. Edith Massey plays the 'Queen', another term from the vocabulary of gay subculture denoting effeminate gay men embodying demanding and spoiled femininity in a flaming performance. Massey herself was a former barmaid and thrift-store owner in Baltimore's harbour neighborhood Fells Point, and her beehive hairdo and a voluptuous body in sexy tight outfits cite the out-of-date and cheap sexualised fashion of the white-collar town that continues as a trace in Waters' role as John, the thrift-store owner on *The Simpsons*.

Desperate Living imported the alternative erotic fetishes of B-movie traditions, heavy-set or older women and urban sexual subcultures, such as strip clubs and gay leather bars, into independent cinema. Trash cinema, including B-movies and sexploitation, subordinates narrative and aestheticisation to a fetish spectacle of sexual deviance. Thus, the lack of characters' psychological interiority and narrative coherence in Waters' films celebrates the tradition of its sources, but the ironic decontextualisation turns the spectacles into camp. Waters expresses his love for artifice in his own hyperbolic way: 'I hate reality, and if I could have my way, everything I captured on screen would be fake – the buildings, the trees, the grass, even the horizon' (1995: 167).

Lesbians and Sexploitation

Desperate Living primarily relied on with female characters, appropriating the tradition of sexploitation to cast lesbians for implied heterosexual, male audiences as erotic objects. In addition, while feminist and lesbian artists were involved in video and art production in the 1960s and 1970s, they did not reach the same kind of global fame, as did for example Warhol (see Butler 2007). Thus, filmic representation of lesbians remained almost exclusively confined to the sexualised genres of B-movies until female experimental filmmakers, such as Su Friedrich in the US, Chantal Akerman in Belgium and Ulrike Ottinger in West Germany radically changed the structures of visual representation in the late 1960s/early 1970s.

Sexploitation continued the tradition of the social-educational film from the Weimar Republic that gave audiences the illusion of privileged and non-prurient access to a social group that otherwise remained invisible in dominant society. Those films created titillating images for voyeuristic audiences but at the same time also provided limited access to a distorted mirror for spectators looking for self-recognition. Joseph P. Mawra directed *Chained Girls* in 1965 for producer George Weiss, who also financed *Glen or Glenda*. *Chained Girls* takes the format of a documentary, with an authoritative male voiceover laid over images of street scenes from Greenwich Village in New York City, intercut with footage of a female photographer setting up a photo shoot of a woman in the process of undress. The voiceover asks rhetorical questions, such as 'What is lesbianism?', provides a brief historical account that returns to Sappho and the island of Lesbos, and gives statistics and psychological explanations for lesbianism (such as 'alcoholic or psychopathic fathers'). A faux ethnographic account outlines the subcultural slang for the different roles taken on by lesbians, such as 'butch or dyke', 'stomping butch' or 'baby butch'.

The documentary and ethnographic conventions thinly disguise the film's salacious portrayal of lesbians that hinges on the pairing of sexuality and violence. *Chained Girls* presents the figure of the dyke as predatory lesbian, repeatedly undressing photo models, with a propensity toward violence. The voiceover describes how 'gangs of baby butches with fists, lead pipes and chains' attack strangers in the street. The narrative high point is the 'coming out party' for a 'baby dyke' who is ravished by a group of lustful and predatory 'butches'. The film repeatedly intercuts reenacted sex acts between women in different stages of undress with minimal narrative continuity and coherence, creating a thin layer of an educational narrative over visuals of sexualised women intended to titillate an audience.

Yet toward the latter half of the decade, the gap between sexploitation and mainstream feature films began closing. B-movies with lesbians were made with higher production value and artistic quality, still in the realm of softcore or X-rated. The late 1960s experienced a 'golden era' of softcore in 'a decentralized circuit of drive-ins, grind houses, and art houses' (Andrews 2006: 61). The presence of repeated simulated sexual spectacles defines feature-length films as 'softcore' and determines their rhythm by appearing in regular intervals. David Andrews suggests that softcore in its 'mainstream form' favours female nudity so that same-sex 'girl/girl' numbers do not detract from its built-in heterosexism (ibid.). The B-movie category of 'awakening sexuality' featured prominently in softcore, and Radley Metzger's *Therese and Isabelle* exemplifies this type (2006: 74). Richard Corliss, however, in the film journal *Film Quarterly*, suggests that *Therese and Isabelle* 'transcended its genre' of the 'sex exploitation film' by appealing to both 'snobs and slobs' because of its 'lesbianism, artful direction, art-house pretensions, suggestiveness and a respectable literary property' (1968: 64). At the same time, the film follows its generic formula, showing sex scenes every ten minutes after the onset of the girls' first sexual encounter, including an extensive masturbation scene.

The narrative follows the memory of a grown-up Therese, who returns to the French all-girl school she attended as a teenager. The film moves back and forth between the past and the present, unraveling the erotic love story between Therese and Isabelle with flashbacks within a flashback. The narrative begins with a secret meeting between Therese and Isabelle, as schoolgirls, in a bathroom stall overdetermined by their melodramatic dialogue: 'Say it!' 'Kiss me … on the mouth' 'I hate you!' Their relationship ends when Isabelle's parents pick her up, leaving Therese behind. The film relies on sexual fantasies about Catholic school girls that invert the repression of sexuality within Catholicism. The film evokes *Girls in Uniform* in its sparse setting and the centrality of the staircase where Therese and Isabelle encounter each other and which represents the threshold Therese has to cross to visit Isabelle at night. Therese's voiceover tells the story, which dominates especially during the sex scenes.

The film addresses both straight male and lesbian audiences with different filmic strategies. The sex scenes that punctuate the narrative are non-explicit in their visual representation. Instead of sex acts, the film shows poses of female nude bodies in embrace or their faces registering sexual excitement. At the same time as the female bodies are offered as erotically aestheticised objects, the voiceover describes their sexual encounters in explicit terms in extended passages that evoke the film's literary source by Violette Leduc. For example, in the last sex scene both women lie naked between trees, while Therese's voiceover narrates explicit acts in the first person: 'I made my way inside ... I was stretched open as wide as my tights ... I felt her secret lips ... my anus ... the timid finger entered me...' This split between visual and sound claims good taste and artistic value by offering an explicit sexual narration through the voiceover that is, however, not accompanied by equivalent images. The obvious older age of the actresses who play the girls, part of the low quality of the film, invites a sexualised, voyeuristic gaze at the girls. Their obvious maturity, however, does not capture memories of lesbian first love, which would focus on the insecurity of sexual exploration, and the danger and vulnerability associated with non-normative desire for young girls. The film's reliance on the genre of the memoir, searching for the ghosts of the first hidden love, looking for its traces in a building, in which characters and emotions come to life, reflects an understanding of lesbian love that privileges returns to past trauma of loss over imagining a utopian future.

Robert Aldrich's *The Killing of Sister George* (1968) similarly frames its lesbian characters in the paradigms of deviance. Based on a play by Frank Marcus, it became, according to Boze Hadleigh, 'America's first X-rated film with a legitimate cast' (2001: 53). It portrays the claustrophobic lesbian relationship between June, who goes by the name of 'George' after the character 'Sister George' whom she plays on a British soap opera, and Alice, her younger, attractive lover, who goes by Childie. George's television character Sister George dies on the show, George's relationship with Childie deteriorates, and Marcy Croft, the BBC executive who delivers the news of her character's 'impending death', steals Childie away from her. The film focuses on the humiliation of George's vulnerable masculine pose.

Similar to other films, *The Killing of Sister George* mobilises gay and lesbian tropes that discredit lesbians but also create a limited recognition within that distortion. Most importantly, the film portrays a butch/femme relationship but exaggerates it to the degree of pathology. *The Killing of Sister George* caricatures the subcultural life style of lesbian butch/femme couples between the 1930s and 1960s (see Kennedy & Davis 1993). *The Killing of Sister George*'s image of lesbians comes close to a monstrous existence particularly that of butch George, emphasised by the horror music score, while sexualised Childie wears different teddies in pink and baby blue. In the absence of butch/femme representation in a larger cultural context, however, those images offered a distorted mirror to lesbians looking for self-reflection.

The film endows the dynamic of butch and femme with a perverse power play that invites voyeurism, while it authenticates its portrayal of lesbian life through a scene set in an actual gay bar in London. In a key scene, George and Childie act out their dominant/submissive relationship when jealous George ritually punishes Childie by forcing her to kneel at her

Robert Aldrich's *The Killing of Sister George* (1969); the authentic lesbian bar

feet and chew a cigar. When Childie does this with great pleasure, she subverts George's desire for domination. Similar to the evocation of the social organisation of subculture in butch and femme, the film also includes a scene of an 'authentic' lesbian bar in London, Gateways, when George and Childie participate in the lesbian community (see Hadleigh 2001: 54). Film scholar Kelly Hankin suggests that scenes in lesbian bars serve to authenticate a subculture and alleviate anxiety for directors about speaking for a subcultural group to which they do not belong (2002: 79).

Chained Girls, Therese and Isabelle and *The Killing of Sister George* show traces of the subcultural lives of lesbians but turn those into images of sexualised and monstrous deviants that titillate by breaking taboos. Their hyperbolic representation allows the films to be read as camp but at their time, lesbians often experienced them as hurtful denunciations, revealing a generation gap between those who lived through this particular repression of gays and lesbians and those who came of age later.

This chapter shows how queer aesthetics constitutes an important meeting point between trash and high art. The following chapter illustrates that the development of an out gay and lesbian politics moves the representation of homosexual characters into the mainstream, radically changing their representation. When queer audiences are not dependent on trash cinema to see their distorted images reflected, the significance of sexploitation and B-movies wanes and with it the pleasure of camp. With the development of a home video market and internet porn, the consumption of films about sexual deviance disappeared from red-light districts, harbour neighborhoods, and sleazy and cheap back-alley movie houses first into living rooms and then into cyberspace. When the sexualised, monstrous, horrific, sleazy and exaggerated melodramatic queer figures on the margins of film culture vanished, a culture of experimentation was lost as well. Outrageous performances broke bourgeois taboos, tested boundaries of taste and constituted a queer aesthetic. The next decade brought positive gay and lesbian characters out of the closet and into the mainstream, leaving behind their queer and campy forerunners.

STONEWALL AND THE POSITIVE
    IDENTIFICATION FIGURE

In June 1969 frequent police raids on gay bars ignited a two-day fight between drag queens and the police at the Stonewall Inn in New York's Greenwich Village. Film titles, such as Greta Schiller and Robert Rosenberg's *Before Stonewall* (1984) and John Scagliotti's *After Stonewall* (1999), signify the event as a watershed moment, separating gay and lesbian history into a 'before and after'. 'Before' stands for the homosexual subculture, associated with bars, double life, coded language and role play, and 'after' implies contemporary politicised gay and lesbian identities, associated with 'being out', pride and demands for equal rights.

The post-Stonewall gay and lesbian movement in the late 1960s and the 1970s occurred in the context of international political movements. Since that time, '1968' has become shorthand for the international student protest movement against the Vietnam War, various anti-colonial liberation struggles and the civil rights movement in the US, all of which set the stage for the second women's movement to emerge in the 1970s. Second-wave feminism claimed lesbianism as a political choice to undo patriarchy. The slogan, 'Feminism is the theory; lesbianism is the practice', which circulated in the early 1970s, captures the politicisation of sexual desire, spelled out by Anne Koedt: homosexuality 'challenges a cornerstone of sexist ideology' (1973: 256).[1] These new ways of thinking about the relationship among politics and identity, ideology and desire, theory and practice were not immediately reflected on the big screen, in part because of the high production cost of film. The effects of feminist lesbianism and the generational shifts from pre- to post-Stonewall male gay culture appear in films throughout the 1980s and were soon overshadowed by the emerging AIDS crisis.

During the two decades from the late 1960 to the late 1980s, Hollywood underwent its own, albeit related, transformation, adjusting to the changing political and cultural climate. The production code gave way to a new rating system by 1968. The studio system began failing at the end of the decade because television stations stopped acquiring films to broadcast (see Bordwell & Thompson 2008). Films of the so-called New Waves from West Germany, France, Japan, India and Eastern Europe showed American audiences a modern vision produced by individual *auteurs* shot in real, often urban, locations and with small budgets. Hollywood's epic tragedies and light-hearted musicals could no longer satisfy the changing tastes of its audiences.

In response, Hollywood produced 'counterculture-flavored films aimed at young people' by a new generation of filmmakers called the New Hollywood (Bordwell & Thompson 2008: 464). Instead of moving 'through the ranks of the studio system', those directors – Arthur Penn, Mike Nichols, Dennis Hopper, Francis Ford Coppola, Martin Scorsese, Brian de Palma and Steven Spielberg – attended film schools and were influenced by the European New Waves. The films of the American New Wave, such as Penn's *Bonnie and Clyde* (1967), a story that made heroes out of famous bank robbers, Nichols' *The Graduate* (1967), in which a young man is seduced by a calculating older woman, and Hopper's *Easy Rider* (1969), a counter-culture road movie, capture the period's anti-establishment attitude. Yet the rebellion modeled on these films did not question underlying assumptions of heterosexuality for the sexual and social liberation.

The development from the Hollywood studio system to the New Hollywood directors privileges artistic visions over financial considerations and subversive narratives over conservatives ones. Yet ironically this development was not necessarily advantageous for gay men and women. Since *auteurism* relies on the single vision of the director, it typically privileged individual men in the male-dominated film industry. With only the exception of editors such as Dede Allen and Thelma Schoonmaker, few if any of the major figures associated with 'New Hollywood' were women (and still fewer were openly gay). *Auteurism* consolidated power in the director instead of distributing it across different departments defined by a division of labour, which included areas, in which women and gay men traditionally flourished, such as costume, make-up and set design. 'Many would indeed look back on the studio era with a sense of nostalgia' explains William J. Mann (2001: 366). His book, *Behind the Screen: How Gays and Lesbians Shaped Hollywood, 1910–1969*, conspicuously ends in 1969.

Yet, over time and in the context of a general liberalisation of society, the restructuring of Hollywood allowed for explicit representations of gays and lesbians unthinkable under the production code. Throughout the 1980s, as discussed below, mainstream films integrated gay and lesbian characters devoid of the monstrous sexuality that was attached to them in earlier periods. Audiences could see socially conscious, liberal films that portrayed gays and lesbians in enlightened contexts. A cost, however, was the loss of the diversity of representation found in camp, B-movies and exploitation films, which slowly disappeared throughout the 1980s. Queer cinema throughout the 1980s remained a gendered phenomenon, however, because feminism had redefined lesbianism throughout the 1970s as a political identity, while male homosexuality soon had to confront AIDS. Two trends characterised lesbians on film: one, the predominance of romance, and two, a reflection of political and increasingly academic feminist concerns that led to the investigation of the possibility of the medium film to represent fantasy and desire. Films about gay men increasingly addressed loss and mourning, whether explicitly or implicitly reflecting the awareness of AIDS.

The Accidental Lesbian

In contrast to the sexualised representations of deviance in the earlier periods, a series of love stories throughout the first half of the 1980s emphasised non-threatening lesbian encounters. In Robert Towne's *Personal Best* (1982), John Sayles' *Lianna* (1983) and Donna Deitch's *Desert Hearts* (1985), a white middle-class woman happens to fall in love with a lesbian. Throughout the 1980s gay and lesbian cinema bifurcated according to gender, linking lesbians to feminism and gay men to the emerging AIDS crisis, and relying on deep-seated ideas about gender that determined the filmic representations of lesbian and gay characters. Female characters were shown exploring sex with other women without necessarily embracing lesbian identity or community, reflecting notions of female passivity and fluid emotional boundaries between women. Influenced by feminist discourses of the time, same-sex desire became a response to patriarchy explaining lesbianism to sympathetic audiences.

In *Personal Best*, for example, two high-achieving female pentathletes, Chris Cahill and Tory Skinner, are qualifying for the Olympics. Chris, a young, promising female hurdle runner, coached by her father, meets Tory, a successful, established pentathelete, who helps her get a spot on the team coached by Terry Tingloff. Chris and Tory become sexually involved and move in together, without defining themselves as a lesbian couple, which becomes a source of conflict between them. When Tory tries to help Chris improve her high jump, Chris injures herself, for which the coach blames Tory. Chris moves in with the coach, but then falls in love with Denny, a water polo athlete. The film ends with the qualifying competition for the Moscow Olympic Games. Chris, who is in second place, enables Tory to secure third place, so that both get on the Olympic team, which constitutes the happy ending.

In the wake of 1970s feminism, women could discover sexual freedom without becoming lesbians. Chris's development follows a Freudian trajectory from first being dominated by her father, then moving through a lesbian relationship, finally to become a mature heterosexual adult. The film neither advances a lesbian identity, nor a queer subversion of the terms of desire. Typical of the genre of the sports film, issues of hierarchy, desire and gender are negotiated via athletic competitions. Thus, when Chris and Tory overcome their competition in the end, conflicts of desire and identity fall to the wayside.

The women's movement, the demands for free love and liberated sexuality, and the Stonewall rebellion appear in unrecognisable traces, emptied of explicit politics and enabling a heterosexual voyeurism on female bodies, embodied by female athletes. Nude or partially dressed women populate *Personal Best* with shots foregrounding bare legs and, according to Vincent Canby's review at the time, 'their pelvic regions', which led him to accuse director Robert Towne of 'undisguised voyeurism' (1982: n.p.). The explicit gaze of the camera at the women is also enabled by the lack of sexual tension between the female athletes who project asexual relationships to their own and each others' bodies, oblivious to the possibility of desire circulating among them. Instead, following the script of male 'locker room culture', they tell racist sex-jokes about Asian men when they are sitting in the sauna. Their strong female bodies have weak feminine personalities: Chris cries repeatedly, and throughout the film Chris and Tory apologise to the coach.

The lesbian episode is non-threatening, contained in the happy ending of heterosexual love and homosocial athleticism. The happy ending validates heterosexual closure and endorses a voyeuristic male gaze particularly at the film's star, Mariel Hemingway. The sexualisation of her as an actress who played a bisexual character continues extra-textually in her photo-spread in *Playboy*, including on its cover with the headline, 'MARIEL HEMINGWAY GETS PHYSICAL! AN EXCLUSIVE PHOTO SESSION PLUS SCENES FROM HER DARING NEW FILM, *PERSONAL BEST*' (*Playboy* 1982). While lesbian sex scenes can be mined for their heterosexual appeal in extra-textual circulation, within the film, the lesbian encounters are asexual and immature. The film shows Chris and Tory watching television, arm wrestling and engaging in 'fart jokes'. *Personal Best* presents eye candy for spectators including a straight male audience, while it partakes in a liberal discourse by including characters who engage in lesbian sex without being demonised.

Robert Towne's *Personal Best* (1982)

Non-threatening lesbian desire also characterises *Lianna*, which offers a more pointed critique of the liberal environment of an American college town. Set in a small liberal arts college, the film portrays the seemingly progressive environment as relying on double standards. Lianna is married to a frustrated film professor, Dick, who has affairs with his female students. She takes evening classes from a visiting female professor, Ruth Brennen, who seduces her. When Lianna tells her husband that she is having an affair with Ruth, he throws her out. Ruth does not take her in for fear of ruining her professional reputation. Lianna's confidante, Sandy, stays away from her because she is confused by Lianna's sudden lesbianism and retroactively questions the nature of their friendship. Ruth reveals unexpectedly that she is also involved with her department head at her home institution. Lianna ventures into a lesbian bar alone, meets another patron named Cindy, takes her home, and has sex with her, while Ruth is having an affair with a student. Ruth finally leaves Lianna, who finds her old friend Sandy and cries on her shoulder.

The film's socio-political agenda shapes the depiction of the characters and narrative with a camera that remains distant from the disintegration of Lianna's nuclear family, the loss of her children, Ruth's betrayal, her sexual encounters with other women and the overall deterioration of her life. This kind of sympathetic liberal gaze contrasts with the titillating gaze invited by B-movies, the horrified look at the lesbian monster, or the melodramatic manipulation of *The Children's Hour*. As a result, no matter how politically laudable, the film did not speak directly to lesbians. While it did fairly well at the box office and with critics, it became neither a great financial success nor a cult film among lesbians.

Despite its liberal intentions, *Lianna* relies and reworks older lesbian tropes. The teacher seduces Lianna by giving her individual attention but then puts her in her place because their 'special relationship' cannot be public. As the predatory lesbian, Ruth later reveals that she did not expect Lianna to leave her husband but assumed that they would simply have an affair. *Lianna* offers a positive main character for viewer identification who is stronger than either her husband or her lesbian lover had expected. It does not portray 'inborn' homosexuality but follows the main character's path of self-discovery and self-realisation, values that 1970s feminism popularised. Lianna, as the liberal individualised subject, can immediately articulate her newfound identity and her desires to those around her, in contrast to a subcultural collective understanding of identity. Lianna, the sympathetic main character, ultimately remains alone, tragically, without family, lover and community. She is able to return to her female friend but significantly they unite on a playground without access to an interior setting. The lesbian community and the lesbian-identified women, Ruth and Cindy, do not offer Lianna more than sexual encounters that ultimately remain superficial.

Deitch's *Desert Hearts* follows some of the narrative patterns but its emotional investment in lesbian romance and explicit depiction of lesbian sex addresses lesbian viewers more directly than *Lianna* and *Personal Best*. Consequently, its twentieth anniversary was marked with the preservation of a 35mm print by the Outfest Legacy Project for Lesbian Gay Bisexual and Transgender films, a special DVD edition including additional materials by Wolfe, a production company specialising in LGBT films, illustrating its importance in the queer film community. Also, in contrast to the other two films, *Desert Hearts'* happy ending unites the two main characters, suggesting a continued relationship instead of an isolated encounter or failed affair.

The film is set in 1959, when Vivian Bell, an English Professor at Columbia University, travels to Reno, Nevada, for a six-week stay at a ranch, run by Frances Parker, to finalise her divorce. She encounters Cay Rivers, the daughter of Frances' deceased long-time male lover Glen. Reserved Vivian reveals that she and her husband shared a professional life but had no children. When Vivian and Cay fall in love, Vivian is weary of their age difference and the geographical distance. She is also self-conscious about being seen with a woman in public, while vivacious Cay does not hide her sexual and romantic interest in women. Frances reacts with homophobic jealousy and kicks out Vivian who moves into a hotel in Reno. Cay visits her, and they passionately make love. When Vivian leaves via train, she tries to talk Cay into moving to New York with her, or at least traveling to the next train station. The film ends with both of them on the train leaving Reno.

The film is set in the 1950s, but instead of the repressive cultural and sexual environment traditionally associated with the period, *Desert Hearts* depicts a group of free-spirited characters in the desert. The set design, classic cars and country music suggest a period film. Yet *Desert Hearts* appears strangely outside of time by projecting 1980s sentiments and style onto the 1950s. Cay sports a 1980s haircut and shorts, is 'out', consummates relationships through sex and envisions relationships based on equality, all post-Stonewall ideas about lesbianism.

Desert Hearts accounts for homophobia in subtle and differentiated ways. Instead of a sexist husband or bigoted neighbours, Frances' homophobic response to Vivian results from her own maternal love for Cay and expresses her desire to have Cay to herself. The film acknowledges the slippages of desire between deep friendship, maternal care and lesbian love, while insisting on the specificity of the latter. Cay, the proto-feminist, wild woman facilitates Vivian's self-realisation. The film charts Vivian's liberation in the informal and liberating setting of the desert along the changes of her hair and outfits. Vivian sheds her restrictive upper-class pantsuit for a cowboy hat, pants, boots and loose hair, enabled by the fantasmatic space of the desert, in which social rules of formality do not apply.

Desert Hearts includes a lesbian sex scene, remarkable for its explicitness and 'surprising power' in a mainstream film at the time (see Ebert 1986: n.p.). A dramatic conflict between Vivian and Cay frames the encounter, which takes place in Vivian's hotel room. While Vivian still ruminates about the impossibility of their relationship, Cay has undressed and sits naked in Vivian's hotel bed. Vivian stands in the adjacent room dressed in her robe, while Cay sits in bed naked, a doorway visually separating them in different spaces. After a short exchange, the next shot includes both of them, looking at each other in profile. The scene continues with an extreme close-up of kissing and ends with Vivian on top of Cay, reaching orgasm. The lack of music, minimal editing, no cut-a-ways and heavy diegetic breathing heightens the realism, which breaks the taboo on lesbian sex on screen. The simplicity of the sex scene also emphasises the filmic address of lesbians instead of employing sex in straight softcore or sexploitation for a straight male audience. The scene thus makes a political claim to lesbian visibility and visual pleasure beyond the binary of exploitative voyeurism or asexual normalcy.

Underneath the modern lesbian relationship, however, we find a character configuration that reaches as far back as *Girls in Uniform*. Vivian is a teacher, a maternal figure, and Cay an orphan, a wild child. The film straddles these older models of lesbianism with new ideas of equal, egalitarian, sisterly love, reflected in the tension between the historical setting of the 1950s and the political ideologies of the 1980s. *Lianna*, *Personal Best* and

Desert Hearts were groundbreaking to varying degrees in their incorporation of lesbian desire, sex and identities in mainstream film, expanding its range of topics to include lesbians. In that process the films relied on conventional structure, aesthetics and style in contrast to another set of films made by lesbian directors in the mid-1980s, which explicitly engage with the experimental possibilities of film to address lesbian desire privileging fantasy over identity.

Lesbian Fantasies

Lesbian art-house films departed from traditional conventions of narrative film to engage with the possibility of the medium of film to connect politics and desire. Three lesbian/feminist films from the mid-1980s centrally feature fantasy, albeit in very different ways: Lizzie Borden's *Born in Flames* (1983), Monika Treut's *Treut's Verführung: Die grausame Frau (Seduction: The Cruel Woman)* (1984) and Sheila McLaughlin's *She Must be Seeing Things* (1987). While these films reached smaller audiences, their engagement with cinema, fantasy, psychoanalysis and lesbian desire enabled them to gain an important status in feminist film theory and Queer Film Studies (on Treut, see Knight 1995, Richardson 1995, Case 1996; on McLaughlin, see Lauretis 1991, Butler 1993). The investigation of filmic possibilities to explore and engage fantasy and reality in relation to desire creates a space for the contravention of conventional heteronormative filmic representations. These films search for a cinematic language to speak about psychic life outside of heteronormative assumptions by blurring the boundaries between fantasy and reality in their narratives.

Seduction: The Cruel Woman inserts queer desire in an engagement with the literary works of Leopold von Sacher-Masoch (1836–95) and Marquis de Sade (1740–1814), both important European authors for the modern understanding of fantasy, sexuality and politics. The film updates their literature by creating a contemporary dominatrix, Wanda, who controls her subjects, including Gregor, based on the two main characters from Sacher-Masoch's novel *Venus in Furs* (1871), the paradigmatic novel of masochistic aesthetics. The non-linear film connects different reenactments of scenes from Sade's and Sacher-Masoch's writings. Wanda is in a lesbian relationship with Caren who owns a shoe store. Justine, later called Juliette (characters from two different novels by Sade, played by film director Sheila McLaughlin), arrives from the US and becomes part of Wanda's s/m performers. *Seduction* engages with the literature by Sacher-Masoch and Sade that emphasised fantasies of men dominating or submitting to women and reorganises their narratives to centre on an empowered cruel woman (see also Mennel 2007). It shows lesbian sexuality in the context of other perversions and intervenes in the historical construction of gender and perversion, undoing Freud's long-accepted alignment of masochism with femininity and of sadism with masculinity (see Freud 1995).

Seduction foregrounds the fantasmatic nature of desires particularly those that go against societal norms. Fantasy becomes the setting – both cinematically and psychologically – to engage with power and desire. At some point in *Seduction*, Wanda and her lover Caren drift on a float on the water while they make love. The film depicts the scene with jump cuts that break the 180-degree rule, reminding viewers that they are watching a filmic construction. With its ambivalence about its implied realness, the scene captures the nature of sexual desire. In her house, Wanda and her subjects stage s/m performances for audiences. These scenes externalise power dynamics in erotic relationships that are acted out in highly theatrical performances on stage.

She Must Be Seeing Things similarly engages the medium of film as a site to investigate fantasy and desire within the power dynamics of a lesbian relationship. While *Seduction* takes place entirely in a fantasmatic realm, *She Must Be Seeing Things* realistically depicts the everyday of a contemporary lesbian relationship. The film, however, includes scenes that are ambivalent regarding their status of fantasy or reality. *She Must Be Seeing Things* follows the lesbian couple Jo and Agatha. Jo, a filmmaker, is shooting a film about a young nun, Catalina, who later in life cross-dresses as a man. Agatha reads Jo's diary and develops jealous fantasies of Jo's erotic and sexual encounters with men, without narrative explanation. The film intercuts mundane moments of their everyday lives, consisting of meetings at work, cooking and cleaning the apartment, with scenes of Jo's passionate love-making with different men, without fully assuring the audience that these are Agatha's fantasies.

She Must Be Seeing Things negotiates issues that also were central to feminist film theory. The foundational text of feminist film theory, Laura Mulvey's 'Visual Pleasure and Narrative Cinema', suggests that in Hollywood films, male characters advance the narrative, while female characters interrupt the flow for a moment of 'to-be-looked-at-ness' offered to the male gaze. In this model, the film's male hero stands in for the male gaze, which also constitutes spectatorship (1988: 62). But the presupposition of a male active gaze and female passive to-be-looked-at-ness does not allow for an account for lesbian spectatorial pleasure of women desiring women. Mulvey's original model also did not enable a theoretical accounting for racial, postcolonial and other ethnic differences that predetermined women's relationship to the spectacle.[2]

She Must Be Seeing Things touches on both these concerns. Throughout the film, we see Jo working on her film-within-the-film, 'Catalina'. In one scene, Jo directs her actress to watch a straight couple having sex and change her facial expression from curiosity to excitement. Later Jo shows the clip on a screen to Agatha, who is Afro-Brazilian. The film scene reminds Agatha of the different erotic, jealous and violent fantasies that she had about Jo. The moment of Agatha and Jo watching the scene together provides a model of interracial lesbian spectatorship that captures their desire for each other and cinema's possibility to engage with active lesbian fantasies. Film scholar Teresa de Lauretis emphasises that the film reclaims 'the function of voyeurism by rearticulating it in lesbian terms' (2007: 36).

While *Seduction* rewrites masochism, *She Must Be Seeing Things* reenacts voyeurism, two topics that had been taboo in feminist discourse in the 1970s because they were seen as outgrowth of patriarchal domination. These films endorsed lesbian desire unapologetically but also without suggesting that lesbianism is beyond the dynamics of power, even though it is located outside of heterosexuality. Because a film, such as *Seduction*, situated itself in contrast to the radical feminism of the 1970s by not idealising lesbianism and because of its explicit portrait of s/m, it was embroiled in controversies among feminists and with its funding institutions of the West German government (for an example of radical feminism that advocated for lesbianism to liberate women from patriarchy, see Bunch 2000; for accounts of the controversies around Treut, see Knight 1995; Richardson 1995; Mennel 2007).

Film's fantasmatic possibilities also shape *Born in Flames*, which, however, privileges feminism over lesbianism. The film's fantasies concern the radical feminist discourse around the social concerns of the 1970s. *Born in Flames* portrays a future after the socialist revolution in New York, where radical lesbians own radio stations. Women on bicycles come to aid women who are attacked or harassed on the streets of the city. Political activist Adelaide Norris travels to former colonised countries to establish alliances and buy arms for the violent struggle in the US. Politically active groups, such as the Women's Army and a socialist collective at a newspaper, discuss strategies to solve societal problems and questions of coalition building. The FBI arrests Norris, who then dies in jail. In response, the different feminist and socialist organisations join forces. When the two radio stations burn, the radical women's organisations take over a television station and broadcast suppressed information about Norris's death.

The film radically breaks with Hollywood conventions by not offering a narrative about individual desires or figures of identification. Some of the characters are lesbians, which in this film translates into a political commitment to women, such as activism against violence against women, fight against racism, concern for welfare for mothers and participation in anti-colonial struggles and liberation. The multiple characters are concerned with the revolution against all forms of oppression of women. Butchness does not function as a signifier in a configuration of lesbian desire but as an embodiment of revolutionary activity. Collectivity also characterised the film's production. Actresses include Florynce Kennedy, an outspoken African-American lawyer, who defended the Black Panther Party and co-founded the Feminist Party; Katherine Bigelow, who later became known for action films with strong female characters; Sheila McLaughlin, director of *She Must Be Seeing Things*; gay actor and performance artist Ron Vawter; Joel Kovel, an eco-socialist psychiatrist; and Valerie Smaldone, a radio personality.

Born in Flames advances the radical possibility that politics can fuel desire and fantasies of a better, socially just future. The characters engage primarily in discussions about their political activism and the strategies to advance the goals of radical feminism and socialism. The film thus attempts to participate in the feminist debates at the time. Conventions of neo-realism, such as lay actors of the multi-cultural cast, on-location shooting and documentary footage in a narrative located in the future, invert conventional cinematic traditions of fantasy and realism. The film's image of lesbianism registers the imperatives of the radical second women's movement emphasising the refusal of the heterosexual contract in a fight against patriarchal, racist class exploitation. Lesbianism as affective, sexual and emotional attachment to other women takes a backseat to the commitment to the political struggle, however, primarily for women.

Born in Flames, She Must be Seeing Things and *Seduction* engage with the cinematic possibilities of representing non-normative desires infused by feminist politics. Lesbians, however, were also central in love stories that addressed a liberal audience in mainstream, yet independent, cinema. In these films – *Personal Best, Lianna* and *Desert Hearts* – a woman fell in love with another woman but did not necessarily identify as lesbian or became part of the lesbian community. All of these films, however, included main characters that are positive identification figures.

Cinematic Mourning

Queer films of the 1980s were segregated along gendered lines. Films about gay men reflected the changes of homosexuality brought on by the Stonewall rebellion and began to confront AIDS. Paul Borgart's *Torch Song Trilogy* (1988) and Bill Sherwood's *Parting Glances* (1986) portray two different generations in the second half of the 1980s and offer two diametrically juxtaposed responses to the AIDS crisis. While the former looks back melancholically at a formation of gay identity in the moment of its disappearance – the effeminate, cross-dressing female impersonator – the latter radically situates itself in the moment of the mid-1980s. These distinctly different films share the concern with mourning the loss of a loved one, evoked, I suggest, by the AIDS crisis.

Torch Song Trilogy tells the story of a gay life covering the period from the 1950s to the 1980s. Based on a Broadway play by Harvey Fierstein, the film follows Arnold from Brooklyn in 1952 to New York in 1980 and registers the effects of Stonewall, but neither mentions it, nor AIDS. The film pays melancholy homage to the art of transvestism in the portrayal of Arnold's work as female impersonator, a drag queen. As a child in 1952 Arnold dresses up in his mother's clothes. Later, as a young man in Brooklyn, he falls in love with Ed, an avowed bisexual who does not introduce Arnold to his friends, has a relationship with a woman and then leaves him. In 1973, Arnold meets Alan, a young, attractive man; they fall in love and plan to adopt a child. In 1977, Ed and his wife, Laurel, invite Arnold and Alan to their country farmhouse where Alan has a brief sexual encounter with Ed. Arnold and Alan move into a run-down neighbourhood where Alan is killed by gay-bashers. In 1980 Arnold lives with his adopted son David, Ed is staying with him while he is getting a divorce from Laurel, and Arnold's mother visits. Arnold and his mother argue over his demand that she accept him.

Torch Song Trilogy includes a prologue, which shows Arnold as a little child in his mother's closet, dressed up in her clothes and wearing make-up. Then follows a monologue delivered by Arnold as a grown man in his dressing room, breaking the fourth wall by addressing the film audience. The cut between the sequence of his childhood experience and his putting on make-up to transform himself in his dressing room posits that his cross-dressing results from an innate desire but that the way he articulates it changes over a lifetime.

Torch Song Trilogy integrates a melancholic account of a past with the new out-lifestyle of gay men that includes the possibility of an alternative family. Drag queens were instrumental in ushering in the new era of gay rights but then turned into an emblem of the past during the 1970s. The film validates the coping mechanism of the bitchy drag queen that masks the injury of societal rejection. It also portrays a gay lifestyle that largely disappeared with AIDS, consisting of backrooms in bars, where strangers could engage in anonymous sexual encounters. By showing Arnold working as a transvestite and venturing into back rooms of bars, *Torch Song Trilogy* illustrates the fluid organisation of the subculture.

The film validates drag and camp on the brink of disappearing. The opening monologue positions Arnold in the *mise-en-scène* of the cabaret, the site of transvestitism, of non-politicised gayness that entertains. Scholar of Queer Film Studies Matthew Tinkcom suggests that camp forms a strategy of 'critique *and* pleasure' employed by 'dissident sexual subjects' (2002: 4); camp was traditionally associated with cheapness, work-as-play, performance, misuse and nostalgia in contrast to value, labour and history. Tinkcom intervenes in this debate to argue that camp is productive based on the definition of labour as an 'ongoing, repetitive, dull task' but 'work' as that by which 'humans create for themselves something recognizably outside of themselves' (2002: 11). The drag queens' performances constitutes work that they perform live, beyond technological reproduction.

Torch Song Trilogy celebrates the culture of drag queens after the Stonewall rebellion birthed the figure of the modern gay man who did not rely on codes, including effeminacy. Drag seemed to belong to a forgotten era, until it reappeared with a new queer culture in the next decade (see

Paul Bogart's *Torch Song Trilogy* (1988)

the next chapter for a discussion of the revalorisation of drag queer theory and film; for the phenomenon of drag kings, see Halberstam and Volcano 1999). The three drag queens are older, their costumes old-fashioned, and their songs evoke a bygone era, for example, Cole Porter's 'Love for Sale'. The film's title plays on the Joan Crawford vehicle, Charles Walters' *Torch Song* (1953), a story about a Broadway singer, billed as 'Crawford – The Eternal Woman'. Joan Crawford performs hyperfemininity that drag turns into camp through the incongruous performance by the male body, pointing, however, to the original performative nature of gender. Tinkcom suggests that camp productively recuperates the past in a historical consciousness that nostalgically focuses on its pain, as it does in this film (2002: 14).

In his work Arnold produces camp and in his domestic life he embraces kitsch, both of which 'share a fascination with the bad object of consumption', though they are not identical (Tinkcom 2002: 5). *Torch Song Trilogy* highlights Arnold's love of kitsch the first time that Alan stays over at his house. Arnold offers him breakfast and the camera centres on the breakfast table, on which the dishes are decorated by porcelain 'bunnies'. The motif of the 'bunny' links Alan to Arnold but also Arnold to his mother. Early on Alan brings Arnold a little stuffed bunny as a gift. He does not look down on Arnold's outdated sentimentality. Understanding Arnold's desire to be loved, Alan responds by having a radio show play a song for Arnold on their anniversary.

Kitsch connects mother and son but they are both tragically blind to what links them to each other. Despite the societal acceptance of gay parenting, Arnold still yearns for acceptance from his mother. The film's final sequence shows us female light-blue house-shoes with bunnies in a close-up that reveal Arnold in an apron, picking up his adopted son David from school. Later when Arnold argues with his mother at home, we see that she wears the same bunny house-shoes in white, situating Arnold and her in the same relationship to kitsch. The torch song, a song about unrequited love, captures Arnold's unrequited loves, which ultimately refers to his relationship to his mother, defining the film as maternal melodrama between mother and gay son. According to film scholar Thomas Elsaesser, melodrama revolves around family relationships and the 'more intellectually demanding forms of melodrama' focus on the 'interiorisation and personalisation of primarily ideological conflicts' (1991: 70, 71).

The film parallels the melancholia in the representation of disappearing expression of gay life with the mourning of Alan after he is killed. The final conflict between Arnold and his mother concerns the societal, religious and personal validation of mourning, here of Arnold's loss of Alan. And while AIDS is absent, the film is nevertheless centrally concerned with the validation of mourning loved ones in gay relationships, the affective issue in the times of AIDS that could not be addressed by a homosexual rights discourse. While the film mourns the loss of the gay lover and the lack of acceptance by the mother, it melancholically relies on a camp subtext about Joan Crawford, celebrates female impersonation of a gay culture that reaches back to the cabaret of the Weimar Republic, and portrays the pre-AIDS culture of bar back rooms. Yet the narrative also looks forward to a possible future of the gay teenager David.

Whereas *Torch Song Trilogy* nostalgically evokes the past and projects hope into the future, *Parting Glances*, though directed two years prior, is squarely situated in a present of the mid-1980s populated primarily by young gay men. Bobby and Mike, in their late twenties, have been together in a long-term gay relationship. Bobby works for an international health organisation and is leaving for a couple of months to work abroad. His gay boss, Cecil belongs to an older generation with a different gay lifestyle. A married man, he travels to Third World countries where he engages in gay sex. Bobby's and Mike's life contrasts with Nick's, Mike's former boyfriend, who has AIDS. Members of the circle of friends enquire about Nick, but only Mike visits him daily. At the centre of the film, which spans two days, is a farewell party for Bobby, at which different characters come together. Toward the end of the film, Bobby returns home instead of leaving on his trip abroad, while Mike searches for Nick, who went to the beach.

The film situates gay culture squarely in the present dominated by popular mass culture. Nick excessively consumes mediated popular culture. His bedroom has several television sets stacked on top of each other that play MTV, while he listens to opera with head phones. Mike expresses his deep friendship with Nick by buying records for him. Nick negotiates his relationships with electronic communication technologies, watching television and listening to music, talking to his friends on the telephone, and taping his will with a video camera. The film pokes fun at the melodramatic excess of camp through a story Mike is editing. The manuscript of gay melodrama science fiction simply appears as bad taste without a redeeming quality. At the party a woman in a black leotard with extensive tattoos dances among the party goers, reminiscent of 1920s expressive dance. The fact that her partner has a German accent and speaks hyperbolically without making sense, situates them closer to the American comedy show Saturday Night Live's 'Sprockets' sketch featuring Dieter, which poked fun at German coolness with men dressed in black turtlenecks, than to New York performance art around pop art icon Andy Warhol.

The film captures the ambivalence of gay normalcy of the late 1980s when following the AIDS crisis, sex with multiple partners became deadly. Bobby and Mike embody the 'normal' – out and monogamous – gay life possible almost two decades after Stonewall. But normalcy also creates boredom: Bobby claims that he is leaving for his job-assignment because the relationship has become stale. Nick meets Peter, a young gay man who was trying to pick up Mike, at the party. Nick describes the gay life in New York of the late 1970s and early 1980s. Under the shadow of the AIDS crisis, history is reduced to memory of one generation. Parting Glances' director, Bill Sherwood, died four years after its completion of complications from AIDS, leaving this as his only film.

Parting Glances inscribes homosexuality into the emerging popular mass culture of MTV, video and pop music, whereas *Torch Song Trilogy* captures transitions of gay culture throughout twentieth-century America by chronicling one life. Ironically, avoiding the AIDS crisis enables the latter film to create a broader view that does not divide the history of homosexuality in utopian sexual promiscuity before and repressed sexuality after AIDS. *Torch Song Trilogy* emphasises gay cultural expressions at the brink of disappearing, such as camp, kitsch, live performance of transvestism, female impersonation and self-depreciating gay humour. It documents transitions and overlaps of gay culture throughout twentieth-century America; *Parting Glances* claims the influence of homosexuality on contemporary mass-produced American popular culture.

Torch Song Trilogy and *Parting Glances* share with *Personal Best*, *Lianna* and *Desert Hearts* the inclusion of gay and lesbian characters in films based on conventional narrative strategies. *Personal Best* and *Lianna* only allow for gay and lesbian episodic encounters, while the other films portray relationships that continue, including the desire for a family. Tragically, the emerging AIDS crisis pushed the concern with death to the forefront.

In conclusion, the normalising discourse about gays and lesbians in Hollywood films discussed in this chapter, from *Personal Best* to *Parting Glances*, told stories about accidental lesbians who leave behind bourgeois lives, and gay men who live across the watershed of the Stonewall Rebellion, as in *Torch Song Trilogy*, or engage in the new normal queer culture, while mourning those lost to AIDS, as in *Parting Glances*. The next chapter shows how New Queer Cinema in the early 1990s expands in transnational cinematic practices and returns to access the earlier forms of queer cinema, such as camp, queer murderers and the black-and-white aesthetics of the 1920s and 1950s.

4   NEW QUEER CINEMA: A NEW AESTHETIC LANGUAGE

'New Queer Cinema', the title of an essay by journalist and film scholar B. Ruby Rich, first published in 1992, captures the sense of a radical political and aesthetic shift in films that appeared between 1990 and 1992. Derek Jarman's *Edward II* (1991), Christopher Münch's *The Hours and Times* (1991), Tom Kalin's *Swoon* (1992), Gregg Araki's *The Living End* (1992), Laurie Lynd's *R.S.V.P.* (1992), Isaac Julien's *Young Soul Rebels* (1991), Todd Haynes' *Poison* (1991), Jennie Livingston's *Paris is Burning* (1990), Marlon Riggs' *Tongues Untied* (1989) and Gus Van Sant's *My Own Private Idaho* (1991) appeared in this two-year span at film festivals from Toronto to Amsterdam and Park City, Utah (see Rich 2004: 15–18). The films' attitudes radically broke with familiar cinematic representation of gays and lesbians.

The films of New Queer Cinema share an attitude but their aesthetics cover a range from 'imperfect' cinema with low-budget hand-held cameras to sophisticated black-and-white compositions evocative of silent film from the 1920s. The films' breaking of the rules of continuity and disinterest in linear narratives continue the avant-garde traditions of queer filmmakers and artists, such as Andy Warhol, Rainer Werner Fassbinder and Kenneth Anger. The figures of sexual outlaws invoke the work of pioneering gay writers, such as Jean Genet, and filmmakers, such as John Waters.

Low-cost and technological innovation made video available for political activism, performance art and the cinematic engagement with older films. In contrast to celluloid, which has to be developed before it can be shown, video entails the possibility of immediate feedback, used in performance and installation art. Video also opened up the possibility to cut and manipulate older film and television clips. It provided affordable artistic possibilities for video makers to use the medium to manipulate canonical films to excavate their queer subtexts. Cecilia Barriga's 14-minute short film *Encuentro entre does Rainas* (*Meeting of Two Queens*) (1991) splices together different clips from Greta Garbo's and Marlene Dietrich's films to create a fantasy love story between the two lesbian icons, and Mark Rappaport's *Rock Hudson's Home Movies* (1992) rereads Rock Hudson's film appearances for their gay subtext. These two videos bring to the fore the sexual subtexts surrounding Hollywood stars to create a gay and lesbian film history, but they also reflect on the dynamics of desire, fantasy and identification integral to cinema. Video became associated with the convention of the direct audience address based on the practice of video diaries, for example in *Rock Hudson's Home Movies*, *Tongues Untied*, Gregg Araki's *Totally F***ed Up* (1993) and Cheryl Dunye's *The Watermelon Woman* (1996).

The low production cost of independent cinema also led to black-and-white film stock for feature-length films, as in Rose Troche's *Go Fish* (1994) and Gus Van Sant's *Mala Noche* (1986). Lack of resources determined the use of lay actors, as in *Totally F***ed Up* and led directors to forego accurate and consistent period costumes in historical dramas, as in *Edward II*. Individual filmmakers became famous for films made with unconventional cameras: Sadie Benning worked with a Fisher-Price Pixelvision camcorder, when she made her films *A Place Called Lovely* (1991), *It Wasn't Love* (1992) and *Girl Power* (1993). Lack of funding encouraged the production of shorts. Several of the filmmakers associated with New Queer Cinema, Benning, Dunye, Su Friedrich and Pratibha Parmar, were well-known for their short film oeuvre before they made features films.

New Queer Cinema, for example, Jarman's *Edward II*, Kalin's *Swoon*, Haynes' *Poison* and Isaac Julien's *Looking for Langston* (1989) manipulate and refract an earlier cinematic aesthetic through a contemporary lens. Dunye in *The Watermelon Woman* mixes a contemporary hip lesbian love story, set in Philadelphia, with a reflection on the invisible history of African-American lesbians. Excerpts from an old black-and-white 'race film', reproducing African-American stereotypes, are reenactments.

Instead of bemoaning the lack of African-American lesbian film history, *The Watermelon Woman* creates a comedy, recreating an invisible past in a faux video documentary.

New Queer Cinema ties deviant sexual desire to an explicitly different cinematic aesthetics. 'Queer' appropriates the derogatory term but also opens up identity categories, such as gay and lesbian, to include the range of non-normative sexual desires and behaviours. In contrast to the terms 'gay' and 'lesbian' that define clearly demarcated sexual identities, 'queer' allows activists, theorists and filmmakers to expand the range of identities to include gay, lesbian, bisexual, transsexual, intersex, s/m and transgender. However, queer also signifies the deconstruction of identity, proposing that its very notion relies on a bounded coherence that imposes exclusions and limitations on subjectivity. Thus, New Queer Cinema portrayed and investigated desires and behaviours more so than focusing on identity.

New Queer Cinema's unapologetic 'in-your-face-attitude' connects its diverse films and also links it to queer activism of the 1980s. The outrage about the public response to the AIDS crisis, which had begun in the early 1980s, but reached pandemic dimensions among gay men, especially in the United States, during the late 1980s, turned a large number of gays and lesbians into activists and led to the 1987 founding of ACT UP, the AIDS Coalition to Unleash Power. In response to the AIDS crisis, during which older forms of violent discrimination of homosexuals surfaced, ACT UP engaged in public spectacles of civil obedience and commanded media attention to demand access to experimental medications. ACT UP's slogan 'SILENCE = DEATH' endorsed a radical claim of 'being out' that politicised gays and lesbians as a means of survival. The forms of activism, such as 'die-ins' and 'kiss-ins', moved the issue of death and sexuality to the forefront. Protests took 'queer' forms, moving away from traditional marches and demonstrations to interrupt the normalcy of daily lives. The later Queer Nation, founded in 1990, and Lesbian Avengers, founded in 1992, also engaged in political activism organised around the unruliness of desires emphasising coalition and community on the one hand and the disruption of the status quo on the other.

New Queer Cinema emerged from a confluence of political, economic and artistic factors associated with the AIDS crisis and the political activism is provoked. Yet no particular initiating moment, such as the Stonewall riots, or endpoint, such as Hitler's rise to power in 1933 Germany, marked its beginning or end. It therefore defies a clear periodisation. Consequently, following the lead of Rich, this chapter posits 'the moment' of the emergence of New Queer Cinema as a phenomenon most forcefully experienced in 1990–92 but does not limit the discussion to that particular moment, those filmmakers or specific films. For a significant number of filmmakers – Isaac Julien, Gregg Araki, Tom Kalin, Todd Haynes, Marlon Riggs, Jennie Livingstone – the making of their first films coincided with 'the moment' of New Queer Cinema. Even though this was not the case for all the filmmakers whose films fit the political and aesthetic characteristic of New Queer Cinema, it nevertheless created a perception of a new generation.

The chapter's first section on the embrace of outlaws in the films of New Queer Cinema gathers a set of films that portray disempowered immigrants, young hustlers, alienated youth, drug-dealers, poor drag queens and those infected by AIDS as main characters in the films by Gus Van Sant, Gregg Araki and Jennie Livingston. Particularly, Van Sant's and Araki's films claim the gritty realism of low-budget independent cinema. Haynes' *Poison* intercuts three narratives, each evoking a different genre, one of which pays a homage to Jean Genet and his celebration of the (sexual) outlaw. The other two narrative strands reenact the aesthetics of a 1950s low-budget sci-fi and a television documentary evoking low-budget B-movies (see chapter two). Because *Poison* integrates both the figure of the sexual outlaw and New Queer Cinema's staging of history, it functions as a transitional text to the next section, which discusses queer films that explicitly turn to history and evoke earlier forms of aesthetics.

Poison shares this aesthetic and political strategy with Julien's *Looking for Langston*, Kalin's *Swoon* and Jarman's *Edward II*, all of which interrogate sexual politics in relationship to the aesthetics of queer history and are discussed in the chapter's next section. These films take the form of the postmodern pastiche, which, according to Ingeborg Hoesterey, merge 'horizons past and present' and 'borrow ostentatiously from the archive of Western culture' (2001: xi). In short, history in New Queer Cinema does not appear as a completed project. In the films that return to historical moments and figures, past and present bleed into each other on narrative and aesthetic levels. This interest in cinematic citations of earlier periods continue in the films discussed in the chapter's last section on lesbian love stories, *Go Fish* and *The Watermelon Woman*. The focus in the discussion lies in the rewriting of the love story with an emphasis on queer community and its discontents.

But in 1991, the question of belonging to a body of work that was in the process of being named and defined by artists, journalists and theorists was contested. Rich describes the reception of feminist lesbian filmmaker Su Friedrich at the Toronto film festival in 1991, whose film *First Comes Love*, 'provoked catcalls from its largely queer audience' (2004: 18). Rich muses whether this was 'an aesthetic reaction, since Friedrich returns to a quasi-structuralist mode for her indictment of institutionalised hetero-sexuality and thus possibly alienates audiences accustomed to an easier queer fix?' or whether it was 'because the director was a woman,' and mentions that there was only one other lesbian filmmaker, Monika Treut from West Germany (ibid.). Rich questions the inclusiveness of New Queer Cinema in regard to style and gender. The tension concerning the diversity of gender, race, ethnicity and nationalities continues to haunt discussions about New Queer Cinema: is it an American phenomenon dominated by white males? (See for example Contreras 2004; Jennings & Lominé 2004; Leung 2004; Wallenberg 2004.)

New Queer Cinema was an international phenomenon from the outset, indicated by the film festivals of Toronto and Amsterdam and the presence of international directors, such as British filmmakers Isaac Julien and Derek Jarman, and Monika Treut from West Germany. At the same time, the United States inhabits a position of global cultural hegemony and dominates global definitions of gay identity exemplified in the proliferation of 'pride' around the globe, and film, measured by Hollywood's global dominance. Yet important predecessors of New Queer Cinema made films outside the US, including Rainer Werner Fassbinder in West Germany, who made films such as *Faustrecht der Freiheit* (*Fox and His Friends*) (1975) and *Querelle* (1982), as well as director Stephen Frears and writer Hanif Kureshi in the UK who made the ground-breaking *My Beautiful Laundrette* (1985). In West Germany, Monika Treut had been making explicitly queer films since the early 1980s before the 'invention' of New Queer Cinema. Her films *Die Jungfrauenmachine* (*Virgin Machine*) (1988), *My Father is Coming* (1991) and *Female Misbehaviour* (1992), made between the late 1980s and early 1990s, were set in the queer urban spaces of San Francisco and New York. Expanding our scope beyond 'the moment' of New Queer Cinema allows us to include more international, female and minority directors in a survey of New Queer Cinema (see for example Wilton 1995; Gabilondo 2002; Gopinath 2002; Grossmann 2000; and Kuzniar 2000).

While the question of inclusiveness in regard to race and ethnicity has been raised repeatedly, in 1993 Kobena Mercer declared: 'We are in the midst of a wildly creative upsurge in black queer cultural politics' (1993a: 238). In addition to Afro-British and African-American queer film-makers Isaac Julien, Marlon Riggs and Cheryl Dunye who are discussed in this chapter, Michelle Parkerson, herself a lesbian filmmaker, lists Dawn Suggs, Thomas Harris, Sylvia Rhue, Jacqueline Woodson, Jack Waters, Aarin Burch, Jocelyn Taylor and Yvonne Welbon as emerging black queer film and video artists during the early 1990s (see Parkerson 1993). Films that appeared in the moment of New Queer Cinema, such as Isaac Julien's *Looking for Langston*, Marlon Riggs' *Tongues Untied*, Jennie Livingston's *Paris is Burning*, and Cheryl Dunye's *The Watermelon Woman*, fore-grounded race in their investigations of interracial desire, the limits of community, cross-racial fetishisation and the political dimensions of desire. From our contemporary perspective, New Queer Cinema appears as more diverse than the films that came before or after, but the lack of continued and sustained funding throughout the years following, particu-larly for filmmakers of colour, did not enable a sustained and continued body of work to emerge.

The emergence of queer international films by filmmakers of colour from the early 1990s and thereafter resulted from creative impulses that emerged out of a political climate. In addition, a changed funding struc-ture, in this instance the support of innovate filmmaking by Channel Four, enabled the filmic productivity of queer filmmakers from Great Britain, jump-starting the career of Isaac Julien and Pratibha Parmar, for example. Their films addressed sexual desires as they functioned within the minority communities and intersected with postcolonial racial and ethnic tensions in the UK. Pratibha Parmar's 26-minute film *Khush* (1991), about gay and lesbian desire of South-East Asian men and women, continued the series of shorts that she made throughout the 1980s, which addressed race and ethnicity but not sexuality.

New Queer Cinema was not an isolated cultural or artistic expression. The films engaged with other arts, such as poetry, dance, performance art and photography. During the early 1990s, art developed into an increas-ing political battleground where limitations of freedom of expression were fought out. In the US, funding from the National Endowment of Art (NEA) was revoked for four performance artists, Karen Finley, Holly Hughes, Tim

Miller and John Fleck, subsequently known as the 'NEA 4', when con-servative observers deemed their performances to offend 'standards of decency' (for more about what became known as the 'culture wars', see Stearns 1995). During the same time, repeated public scandals surrounded the sexual photographs by Robert Mapplethorpe, whose work appears in several of the films discussed below. The political stakes in the 'culture wars' were high, and they were fought out in the realm of public art and its representation of (queer) sexuality.

The presence of a queer sensibility and expression across different media, art forms and genres indicates the discursive context of 'queerness' produced by artists, activists, critics and scholars in the early 1990s, which created a common language for these films and their audiences. Less well established art forms became more prominent, such as performance art, as a way to embody pain and desire; photography, which lends itself to address the question of visibility and agency; and poetry, particularly among African-American men, as a means of survival. These different art forms relied on older traditions of feminist performance art, gay subtexts in fashion photography and African-American spoken word poetry (for an example of queer fashion photographer Herbert Tobias *avant la lettre*, see Domröse 2008).

New Queer Cinema functioned in a political and artistic exchange with other queer arts, politics, activism and with queer theory. The queer politics of the 1980s created the ground for queer theory as a new academic field. Its most famous representatives, Judith Butler, Eve Kosofsky Sedgwick and later Judith Halberstam, not only established queer theory as a respectable field of enquiry but also made inroads into traditional disciplines, such as Literature, Drama, Political Science, History, Philosophy, Rhetoric, Women's Studies, Sociology and, important in this context, Film Studies.

Judith Butler's ground-breaking book *Gender Trouble* (1990) intervened in feminist theory's paradigmatic concept of the 'sex/gender system', in which sex (male/female) was seen as the biological foundation for gender (masculine/feminine) as its socialised expression (for the essay that origi-nally coined the term 'sex/gender system', see Rubin 1997). Butler pro-poses that sex itself functions as a linguistic interpretation of biology that can only conceive of two sexes seen as inherently complementary basis of compulsory heterosexuality. According to her, ideologies of heterosexuality call upon subjects to perform gender in a way that partakes in the illusion of the coherence coherence of sex as well as gender. When subjects act in ways that undermine the assumed naturalness of the sex/gender system, their particular gender performance becomes subversive because it points to the performativity that creates gender in the first place. Butler accords cross-dressing and camp key roles in her theoretical model because these kinds of marginal practices exaggerate the performance of sex and gender and thus point to their performativity, undermining their assumed naturalness (see Butler 1990).

In contrast to Butler, Eve Kosofky Sedgwick, in her important book *Epistemology of the Closet* (1990) focuses on literature, proposing that the structure of 'the closet' centrally organises American canonical literature and that homosexuality functions epistemologically differently than other identity categories. Thus, Queer Studies in the early 1990s undertook a double move of validating subcultural practices (drag, cross-dressing and camp, for example) and at the same time 'queering' canonical, dominant culture. This double move of validating the margin and queering the centre created a constitutive relationship between queerness and dominant culture that conceptualised the relationship between gays and lesbians and normative sexualities and their institutional forces fundamentally differently than before.

Queer Studies established a space for the theoretical discussion of the films of New Queer Cinema. The simultaneity of the early academic publications and the emergence of New Queer Cinema strikingly indicates the mutual influence and interdependent development of theory and cinematic production. When *How Do I Look?: Queer Film and Video*, edited by Bad Object Choices, appeared in 1991, it included a range of essays that addressed lesbian and gay film history, questions about pornography, race and safe sex, and the negotiation of feminist film criticism with emerging queer paradigms. Two years later, the collection *Queer Looks* brought together theorists and filmmakers to address queer films from different generations, periods, genres, styles and countries (such as the USSR and the Philippines), including video and film, porno and art house. In its inclusiveness regarding filmic work and directors, the collection presented an expansive and self-reflective approach to New Queer Cinema. Conversely, in one of Queer Studies' earliest collections, *Inside/Out*, edited by Diana Fuss in 1991, six out of the 17 essays address film, indicating the importance of Film Studies for the emerging field of Queer Studies.

Sexual and Other Outlaws

Instead of coming-out stories and tragic homosexuals intended to solicit tolerance, the characters of New Queer Cinema – kings, poets, hustlers and murderers – unapologetically express deviant desires and engage in queer sexual practices in rough and gritty images. Illegal immigrants, drunken poets and a clerk in a nickel-and-dime store for the down and outs are the main characters in Van Sant's *Mala Noche*; two HIV-infected young gay men take an aimless road trip in Araki's *The Living End*; and a group of six alienated young queers share disaffected lives in Hollywood in his *Totally F***ed Up*. These films reflect the immediacy of the moment through the conventions of low-budget film. Livingston portrays equally marginalised subjects in *Paris is Burning* about the subcultural practice of 'vogueing' – a cross between dance and walking the runway – by homeless gay men of colour in the late 1980s/early 1990s in New York. However, her film creates a much more ambivalent relationship between its cinematic apparatus and its subjects through the use of a conventional documentary format.

Van Sant's *Mala Noche* is based on the novel *Mala Noche, Or, If You Coger with the Bull You Get the Horn* (1977) by Walt Curtis, a self-declared Oregon street poet, who was part of the underground poet culture of Portland in the 1970s/80, a cultural scene also captured in the film. Walt, a clerk in a small store for the down-and-out that mostly sells cigarettes and beer, is infatuated with Johnny, a young illegal Mexican immigrant who has just arrived in the city. Johnny does not want to be romantically or sexually involved with Walt, who continues his naïve attempts to befriend Johnny and his friend Pepper. He invites them for dinner, gets Pepper cold medicine when he is sick, and tries to teach them how to drive his car. Walt is a highly ambivalent character, searching for love, friendship and affection, but simultaneously paranoid because he cannot understand them. Johnny is deeply distrustful of Walt's gay advances and disappears, leaving his friend Pepper behind, who then becomes involved with Walt. Walt narrates in a voiceover, so that audiences experience the relationships from his perspective. He finds Pepper emotionally limited because he uses 'his penis like a weapon'. When the police appear in Walt's building, Pepper gets shot and dies. Johnny, who has been deported, reappears; when he hears that Pepper was shot, he writes 'puta' ['puta' literally means 'whore' and is also used to imply 'faggot', as it is translated in the subtitles] on Walt's door and leaves.

The conditions of low-budget filmmaking correspond to the marginal lifestyle of film's subjects. The black-and-white film footage (as in *Go Fish*) is both an aesthetic and economic choice. According to Van Sant's commentary, black-and-white makes the production independent on finding perfect settings: if a colour does not match, it does not need to be painted over (Interview, DVD extra materials, Van Sant). Aesthetically, the black-and-white style of hard lighting with one primary source has the effect of highly staged and stylised composition that emphasises and estranges at the same time. The lack of rehearsing and the on-location shooting captures a sense of immediacy and authenticity, while the high-contrast black-and-white with harsh lighting aestheticises and thus valorises life on the margin of society.

The low-budget, affective, direct cinema of Van Sant does not reflect on the politics of gay desire, fetishisation, poverty and migration beyond the representation of Walt's subjective ruminations. His attitudes are disturbing because he lacks self-reflection and self-awareness. For example, he offers Johnny $15 to sleep with him and in his inner monologue refers to Johnny and Pepper as 'ignorant Mexican teenagers'. Yet the visual representation of their encounters is also haunting because it exposes the impossibility that their desires could be fulfilled. In its political ambivalence, the film carves out a place to show gay male desire that neither follows the formula of fetishisation of young men in gay porn, nor adheres to rules of narrativising desire based on political correctness. Instead, the film captures an articulation of gay desire that is paradoxically innocent and politically corrupt because the characters function in a web of exploitation and domination.

Greg Araki shares some of the qualities of Van Sant's filmmaking but belongs to a younger generation. His early films *The Living End* and *Totally F***ed Up* share Van Sant's low-budget quality but rely on video aesthetics. Instead of an emphasis on lighting and depth as in classic film, the image is flat and repeatedly and intentionally includes technical flaws. In *The Living End*, Jon, a young gay movie critic finds out that he is HIV positive when he takes his first AIDS test. He picks up Luke, a gay hustler who is hitchhiking and who is also HIV positive. Luke tells him that they are different than other people because they have a time bomb inside them and that they are totally free. 'We're the victims of the sexual revolution', explains Luke marking them as having come of age in the shadow of the sexual revolution but with the reality of AIDS. Luke has a gun and kills a homophobic attacker, which leads him and Jon to run from the law on a road trip without destination. Luke's facade of disgust for the 'HIV honky dory life' crumbles, exposing his destructive despair and restlessness, and leads him to attempt suicide while aggressively having sex with Jon. The end shows them in the desolate landscape worn out from their tense inter-personal drama that resulted from the pressures and desires associated with a gay coming of age in the times of AIDS.

Totally F***ed Up similarly claims to represent a generation of young queers in the early 1990s, here alienated in LA. Ironically, the film estranges the landscape of LA when the characters repeatedly walk through empty parking garages, gas stations and warehouses. The characters individu-ally introduce themselves directly to the camera, discussing terms, such as 'sex', 'AIDS' and 'masturbation'. All of them are friends, some are in relationships, and several have random sex. Andy commits suicide when his new love, Ian, betrays him. The film shows the community of a genera-tion who act disaffected in an attempt to ward off the fear and emotion associated with becoming sexual in the face of AIDS, when coming out and having sex carries a deadly threat. The early Araki films share with Van Sant's films the low-budget aesthetics of immediacy and authenticity that captures a moment. The film self-reflexively points to, instead of covering over, that this immediacy has been enabled by video technology.

Paris is Burning differs radically in its aesthetic strategies from Van Sant's and Araki's films, which might explain its cross-over success with a mainstream audience. It depicts a subculture organised not around sexu-ality but the pleasure of performance. The film shows a community of gay men of colour that partake in vogueing in New York and that organise them-selves in 'houses' named after French haute couture, in which gay men take on roles of mothers, fathers and children and thus create alternative kinship structures. The highlight of their social life are balls at which the different houses compete with each other under different categories, such as 'realness', 'nice white girl' or 'successful business man' on an imaginary runway with clothes that they have made or put together. The subjects' dreams come across the screen because the men are given ample space in the interviews to describe their world and their desires. The film relies on a

Jennie Livingston's *Paris is Burning* (1990)

conventional anthropological structure in which intertitles provide terms, such as 'houses', 'balls', 'legend', 'upcoming children', that are illustrated through documentary footage and elaborated upon by talking-heads from the community in their own setting. The film translates subcultural practices for a mainstream audience.

Paris is Burning became subject to a theoretical controversy concerning the position of the white female filmmaker who celebrated gay men of colour on the margin of society without investigating her own implication in the power imbalance at work in her ability to make the film. The film functions within the dynamics of commodification of subcultures at the same time that vogueing subversively appropriates signifiers of commodities that are out of reach for the majority of consumers. Jackie Goldsby points to the limits of the documentary genre in this particular instance: 'The film's form as a documentary ... is inimical to the participants' desire for glamour and mass fame. For example, simply by representing Octavia St. Laurent, the film exposes the fiction informing her "realness". She'll never become the supermodel she hopes to be' (1993: 114). Despite her criticism, Goldsby appreciates that the film exists because of the dearth of images showing the creativity of survival by poor gay men of colour, even though the documentary realism undercuts a possible celebration of this subculture's hyperbolic performance. *Paris is Burning* celebrates a transient subculture that would otherwise lack any kind of visible legacy in American culture, and fame is one of the desires voiced by the film's subjects (see Mennel 2008: 190–4). History and politics neither appear as an explicit discourse, nor as category of analysis in these films, though they are saturated by the politics of their own historical moment. A different set of films in New Queer Cinema turns to history more explicitly depicting a particular moment in the past as deeply interrelated with the early 1990s and capturing this relationship aesthetically.

Postmodern Pastiche: The Queer Aesthetics of History

New Queer Cinema casts history as highly relational to the present by refracting the representation of historical figures and periods through the current moment. The films discussed in this section are connected through their politics and aesthetics. Julien's *Looking for Langston* and Kalin's *Swoon* are highly aestheticised, cinephilic films that return to the moment of the 1920s in content and aesthetics. Jarman's *Edward II* and Haynes' *Poison* turn to historical figures and emphasise aesthetics, albeit in very different ways.

Looking for Langston integrates poetry by Harlem Renaissance poet Bruce Nugent (1906–87) and Julien's contemporary, poet Essex Hemphill (1957–95). The film integrates historical documentary footage showing street scenes in Harlem of the early twentieth century with clips of the Harlem Renaissance artists, Countee Cullen, Bruce Nugent, Alain Locke, Wallace Thurman and Zora Neal Hurston. Wallace Thurman and Bruce Nugent lived together in a house on 267 West 136th Street, the interior of which Nugent painted with homoerotic scenes. The artistic movement of the Harlem Renaissance crossed literature, sculpture, painting, journalism and photography with a 'revolutionary' sensibility that advanced a 'black aesthetic', without catering to a dominant 'white' sensibility by hiding problems within the black community. Several of the important members of the Harlem Renaissance were gay and/or women. Julien's contemporary perspective goes beyond a simple reclaiming of the gayness of the Harlem Renaissance. Both artistic movements – the Harlem Renaissance and queer art and culture – resurrected an aesthetics that derived from the margin and did not pander to dominant culture and included different genres and media because they relied on larger philosophical and political frameworks.

Looking for Langston connects the past with the present. By using the verb 'looking' in its title, the film emphasises an active and personal search for history. The film combines fantasy images that are anchored in the Harlem of the past with beautiful actors fashioned according to the 1920s. The film cites Langston Hughes' famous line of poetry: 'What happens to a dream deferred?' over dream-like images spliced together based on visual associations. With the voiceover's description that states that 'homosexuality was the sin against the race, so it had to be kept a secret, even if it was a widely shared one', the film addresses not only a queer but also particularly a black queer audience.

Looking for Langston creates a visual imaginary to connect the poetry of the Harlem Renaissance poets Langston Hughes and Bruce Nugent with the work of James Baldwin and the contemporary poetry by Essex Hemphill and Hilton Als, who is also a theatre critic. While Julien employs dream-

Isaac Julien's *Looking for Langston* (1989)

Marlon T. Riggs' *Tongues Untied* (1989): Marlon T. Riggs & Essex Hemphill (© Ron Simons/
Image: Filmmuseum Berlin – Stiftung Deutsche Kinemathek)

like images to create a historical continuum of black, gay creativity, Marlon
Riggs' *Tongues Untied* recites Essex Hemphill's poetry in conjunction with
works by black, gay poets Reginald Jackson, Craig Harris, Steve Langley,
Alan Miller and Donald Woods, conjuring up contemporary visual images
that are dynamic and interactive.

   The images in *Looking for Langston* include the erotic black male body
in fantasy landscapes of fields, draped on beds, dancing in bars and restag-
ing anonymous sexual encounters at night. Both films mediate on the 'open
secret' of white men fetishising black men, which was a topic brought to the
surface by the fetishising homoerotic photographs of black nudes by white
photographer Robert Mapplethorpe. Several public scandals in the United
States and the United Kingdom surrounded exhibitions of Mapplethorpe's
sexual photographs in the 1990s, shortly after he died of AIDS. In Queer
Studies, scholars raised the question whether Mapplethorpe's work reproduced or critically reflected upon the fetishisation of black men and the
power of the objectifying dominant gaze inscribed with whiteness (see
Mercer 1991 and 1993b). *Looking for Langston* integrates the erotic photo-

graphs by Mapplethorpe and contextualises them in articulations of desire by gay, black men.

Kalin's *Swoon* similarly returns to the early twentieth century and cinematically captures the aesthetics of the historical moment. Kalin's *Swoon* fictionalises the infamous thrill murder by lovers Nathan Leopold and Richard Loeb, members of upper-class German-Jewish families, of 14-year-old Bobby Frank in 1924 in Chicago (see Higdon 1999). *Swoon* also rewrites film history because the story had been made into a film twice before, once as Alfred Hitchcock's *Rope* (1948) and later as Richard Fleischer's *Compulsion* (1959), both times with a homophobic coding of Leopold and Loeb (for a discussion of *Rope*, see chapter two here, and Miller 1991). Similar to *Looking for Langston*, Kalin integrates documentary footage of Chicago, including clips from the legal proceedings with famous defense attorney Clarence Darrow. The black-and-white film neither follows the linear narrative conventions of feature films, nor the truth claims of documentary films. Interspersed in the documentary footage are black-and-white shots that evoke 1920s cinematic style with extreme close-ups of the main two characters in strung-together episodes.

While *Looking for Langston* creates fantastic imaginary spaces integrating poetry by Langston Hughes and Essex Hemphill to recreate Harlem as a real and fantasmatic place, Kalin frames the story of Leopold and Loeb with stagings and quotations of Sacher-Masoch's *Venus in Furs*. The recurrent interest of New Queer Cinema in variations of sadism and masochism, for example Treut's *Seduction: The Cruel Woman*, Haynes' *Poison*, Araki's *The Living End*, does not reflect liberal inclusiveness of the range of perversions but is instead driven by an interest in the intersection of politics, power and desire, which had been pushed to the foreground by the AIDS crisis. *Venus in Furs* depicts the staging of submission to a dominant woman framed as a fantasy in a diary by the main male narrator before the term 'masochism' was invented in 1890 by sexologist Richard von Krafft-Ebing in his volume *Psychopathia Sexualis* (see Mennel 2007). Masochism as perversion was associated with fantasy, induced by literature. Instead of making an explicit argument about the case of Leopold and Loeb, Kalin subtly suggests that the murder was part of a complex web of power and desire. He inverts the narrative structure of *Venus in Furs*, however, by depicting a historical event with a narrative frame that emphasises fantasy.

Death and loss constitute the narrative core of the two aestheticised films *Looking for Langston* and *Swoon*. The former begins with a eulogy for Langston Hughes, and the latter narrativises a murder. In the time of the making of the films, death – in the form of AIDS – pervaded the gay community worldwide. Both films, as well as *Tongues Untied*, work through the AIDS crisis by turning to other moments of haunting deaths. *Tongues Untied*, for example, opens with a comparison about the significance of crack and AIDS for the black community. Hughes' last poem to be quoted in the film 'I could be blue but I've been blue all night long', captures the camp strategy of survival in a darker shade of black, implying a different history with the connotation of the word 'blue' (as in blues and the 'blue notes' in jazz).

Jarman's *Edward II* shares this interest in homosexuality situated at the nexus of desire and power in combination with a historical legacy of the aestheticisation of camp. King of England, Edward II (1307–27) had a scandalously close relationship to commoner and foreigner Piers Gaveston while he was married to Isabella of France. Alienated from her husband, Queen Isabella left England with her lover, Roger de Mortimer, for the court of French King Charles IV, and from there moved to the French Court in Flanders. There she and Mortimer gathered an army to return to England and in 1326 defeated Edward II. Isabella's son Edward III was crowned at the age of 14, and Isabella and Mortimer became regents. Shortly before his eighteenth birthday, Edward III ordered and succeeded in a coup against Mortimer and Isabella. Mortimer was sentenced to death and Isabella exiled from court.

The film is based not on the actual events but on Christopher Marlowe's (1564–93) play *Edward II*, which gives the dialogue the staged quality of dramatic language and adds a level of distanciation. According to scholar Viviana Comensoli, academic approaches to the play are divided between those 'who see the play as a morality-patterned tragedy inscribing a cause-and-effect relation between a king's "unnatural" love for a male subordinate and social disintegration and those who claim that, while Marlowe may be sympathetic to the love relationship between Edward and Gaveston, the issue of homosexuality is isolated from the sociopolitical context of the tragedy' (1993: 175–6). Comensoli suggests that Marlowe departed from the 'official Tudor history' of his sources, which emphasised the King's inefficiency, to foreground Edward II's homosexuality and the homophobia that drove his punishment. Thus she posits that the play itself already contrasts non-normative desire with heterosexual institutions.

According to Comensoli, Marlowe shows how 'sodomy' undermines the heterosexual structure of institutions of power, basing her interpretation on the works of the anthropologist Claude Levi-Strauss's concept that the exchange of women between men constitutes kinship structures, which applies particularly to early modern England where men negotiate political relationships between them and women function as objects of exchange in marriage.

The film places its action in a bare setting, in which light creates depth and dimension. King Edward II is surrounded by his lover Gaveston and Isabella and Mortimer who are vying for power. *Edward II* retains the quality of the drama by ignoring cinematic continuity, the illusions of continuous space and time created through editing and setting. The dialogue is based on Marlowe's text, whereas the costumes are an eclectic mix referencing past and present. The symbolic acts and exaggerated performances reflect non-realist acting but also accusatory descriptions of Edward II and Gaveston from the time. The film returns to a moment in history, in which homosexuality *avant la lettre* became legible in a coded language of normalised homophobia that has described Edward II as affected with 'ineffectual effeminacy' (Prasch 1993: 1165). The film does not tell a private story – as the liberal view of sexual identity would have it – but situates desire in the context of institutions, such as the church, the military, the police and heterosexual marriage. Thomas Prasch suggests that the film then elevates 'sodomy in Marlowe's play from a subversive subtext to textual centre' (1993: 1164). Jarman follows Marlowe by depicting a 'court life rooted in homoerotic aesthetics' which 'placed the king at odds with an aristocratic and church culture committed to the ideal of compulsory heterosexuality' (1993: 1165).

In contrast to earlier readings of Edward II as an ineffective king, Jarman portrays Edward II and Gaveston in 'community egalitarianism' (ibid.); this, Prasch suggests, contrasts to homophobic institutions including heterosexual marriage, which the film portrays as an 'exercise of power, embodied in Roger Mortimer's taste for sadomasochistic sex ... and Queen Isabella's icy vampirism' (ibid.). Yet Bette Talvacchia criticises the film's rewriting of the role of Queen Isabella, who was married to Edward II when she was 12 years old: 'Jarman never explores a contingent aspect of the story: that Isabella's villainy was largely formed by the same destructive forces of the institution of marriage, and the subjugation of women within its structure' (1993: 124). She points out that the different texts accuse Isabella of adultery with Mortimer, yet that in order for Isabella to oppose her husband effectively, she had to align herself with a man. This blindspot via-a-vis the position of women in the political analysis underlying the representation of the friction between queer desire and dominant institutions marks New Queer Cinema and points to the limits of its political analysis, libratory possibility and the effectiveness of the term 'queer'.

The postmodern pastiche, visible in the simultaneous premodern and modern costumes, settings and behaviours, is particularly emphasised in the encounters between the church and queer demonstrators in leather jackets with signs 'Take your filthy laws of my body'. *The Watermelon Woman, Rock Hudson's Home Movies, Edward II, Swoon, The Meeting of Two Queens* and *Looking for Langston* share the technique that constitutes postmodern pastiche but all are unambiguously political (see also Dyer 2007). Scholar of postmodernism, Frederic Jameson's often-cited definition differentiates pastiche from parody and satire, which are intentionality political, claiming that 'Pastiche is thus blank parody' (1991: 17). Ingrid Hoesterey in her book *Pastiche: Cultural Memory in Art, Film, Literature* departs from Jameson's definition of pastiche in a way that echoes with the political strategies of the films at hand: 'Postmodern pastiche is about cultural memory'; it is part of 'culture beyond a high-low dichotomy' and advances 'emancipatory aesthetics' (2001: xi).

Pastiche's practice of 'neither original, nor copy', an important characteristic of these films, constitutes a queer mode of filmic expression that does not posit aesthetics and politics as juxtaposed to each other or as mutually exclusive. Aesthetics as politics has been the historic domain of gay men, and these films continue that tradition, heightening the aestheticism of a time gone by but also excavating and reflecting on the politics inherent in those aesthetic traditions in the first place.

The New Queer Love Story: Lesbian Community and its Discontents

Looking for Langston and *Tongues Untied* struggle to come to terms with the political imperative 'Black is Beautiful' without reducing black gay men to erotic objects. Lesbian film operated under the weight of feminist film theory that had analysed the 'male gaze' aligned with the male hero who advances the narrative in contrast to woman's 'to-be-looked-at-ness' that arrests the narrative. Laura Mulvey's ground-breaking essay 'Visual Pleasure and Narrative Cinema' had outlined this heterosexually structured gendered organisation of mainstream film and spectatorship, which did not lend itself to capture or theorise lesbian and gay desire on screen. Feminist film theory aimed to destroy the pleasure of looking at women, thereby denouncing the sexual objectification of women claimed to be foundational of mainstream film. As a consequence, earlier feminist-inspired lesbian films would cast lesbian desire as unrepresentable, for example, in Chantal Akerman's film *Les rendez-vous d'Anna* (*The Meetings of Anna*) (1978) (see Mennel 1997). New Queer Cinema's emphasis on female desire for women on the screen worked against dominant society's injunction of representing perverse desire and feminists' objectification to the sexualisation of women. At the same time, the feminist film movement and film theory created the foundation for queer filmmaking (see Rich 1998a).

Troche's *Go Fish* and Dunye's *The Watermelon Woman* share characteristics with the films outlined above: the integration of past and present in the search of a new aesthetic, particularly the inflection of an aesthetics from the 1920s (for example *Go Fish*'s jazz score), the innovation enabled by video, and connections across media with photography, literature and performance art. *Go Fish* integrates aspects of experimental cinema into a cross-over appeal and *The Watermelon Woman* makes the history of racial tensions in the lesbian community the basis of a light-hearted comedy.

This section emphasises New Queer Cinema's radical rewriting of the genre of the love story, a staple of narrative cinema and a preferred genre of the post-Stonewall lesbian films in particular (see chapter three). *Go Fish* and *The Watermelon Woman* shift the model of identification from the couple as in *Desert Hearts*, *Personal Best* and *Therese and Isabelle* to the lesbian community, which, however, is fraught with tensions and limitations. The films present love stories but queer the genre conventions.

Go Fish tells a simple tale: girl meets girl, girl falls in love with girl, girl gets girl. Max falls in love with Ely, whose girlfriend lives in Seattle. They are surrounded by roommates, friends and lovers: Max's roommate Kia, who is African-American and teaches Film Studies and her girlfriend Evy, and Ely's roommate Daria, who has a string of different sexual partners throughout the film, including a man. *Go Fish* portrays mundane everyday life, in which characters negotiate problems associated with being queer, such as being kicked out by their parents or understanding what defines a lesbian. In contrast to the films of earlier periods, the impossibility to 'name' lesbian desire, or conversely to 'come out' does not motivate the narrative. The characters do not suffer tragic fates because of their lesbianism.

The film gestures to the convention of the love story to negotiate a new queer, lesbian identity in the context of community and aesthetics. *Go Fish* interrupts its narrative with associative close-ups and shots of urbanity, a strategy it shares with *Swoon*, *Looking for Langston* and *The Watermelon Woman*. Similar to *Mala Noche*, the black-and-white resulted from a limited budget but increases the film's aestheticism. The intense emphasis on aesthetics of New Queer Cinema, especially in its black-and-white films (*Virgin Machine*, *Swoon*, *Looking for Langston*, *Go Fish*) constitute a particular contrast to the films of the 1970s, breaking with 'the aesthetic conventions of realism and the philosophical sensibility of humanism' (Leung 2004: 155). Associative images of a spinning top, interlocking hands and decaying urban sites interrupt the narrative without providing explicit meaning, creating a space for meditation in the context of community beyond the film. The film negotiates community via style also on the level of its narrative. In a central scene, Ely has her long hair cut off into a crew cut, an extremely short hair cut traditionally associated with masculine men or the military, and is rewarded with positive attention by the others. The characters spend time thinking about their outfits and discussing them with each other. Combat boots, vests, short tops, tight belts, shorts and baseball caps worn backwards make up a style that marks their belonging to the community.

Go Fish connects to lesbian performance art, photography and experimental cinema of the late 1980s to late 1990s, emphasised in one particular vignette that appears late in the film. Max engenders dream-like, meditative episodes; in one of them we hear her in a voiceover reflect on being a lesbian, while she is centred in the shot in a wedding dress. After the next cut, another character stands besides her dressed the same and their friends appear in a row in their usual dyke outfits of jeans and black leather jackets, giving each of them a kiss. Then the two female characters take off their wedding dresses and put them back on. The voiceover thinks out loud about women's expected paths toward marriage. Multiple voices, in part whispered, echo Max's reflections. At the end of the experimental scene we hear Max's voiceover: 'I'm not waiting for a man.'

Queer film throughout the 1990s connected to photography and performance art, part of the creative force unleashed by the AIDS crisis that

Rose Troche's *Go Fish* (1994)

cut across different media. *Go Fish*'s particular sequence is reminiscent of performance art and experimental cinema by stripping the *mise-en-scène* down to an empty loft in a static, straight-on medium-long shot that shows characters that perform on a symbolic and not realist level. The verisimilitude of film has disappeared (similar to the structure in *Glen or Glenda*; see chapter two). The staging of this scene also evokes the unapologetic subcultural style, sexual desire and a direct look into the camera reminiscent of the works by lesbian photographers at the time, such as Jill Posener, Jackie Kay, Della Grace (who continues to make photos as Del LaGrace Volcano) and Tee Corinne who rose to fame in the 1990s. They share with the performance artists, such as Karen Finley and Holly Hughes, the centrality of the female body boldly addressing the camera and by extension the audience.

Posener's staged photos share with *Go Fish* the style of a subculture that embraces fetishes of times past in the accruements of sexualised femininity, such as lingerie and high heels, of sexualised hyper-masculinity, such as leather, uniforms, suspenders, all of which had disappeared under the influence of 1970s feminism because they were seen as signifiers of gendered patriarchal behaviour and roles. By highlighting these sexual signifiers and combining them in incongruent ways, such as combat boots with lingerie, the style foregrounds the agency of those who take on and off these different aspects of sexualised behaviour and create an embodied postmodern pastiche of sex and gender. Butch and femme, the lesbian role play, returned, validated by Queer Studies' emphasis on performativity that argued that butch and femme were not simply reproducing heterosexual roles but expressing a particular articulation of lesbian desire and cultural expression of community (see Case 1993). The subjects in Posener's photos look into the camera with a bold look, similar to the characters in *Go Fish*. Posener's explicit erotic photos that show rough sex and role play by women more radically breaks taboos than the film, which addresses a broader audience and relies on traditional beauty standards. The casting of Guinevere Turner as the main character in *Go Fish* and the love interest in *The Watermelon Woman*, while butch, heavy-set, black female characters occupy the minor roles of the sidekicks in both films, delineates the real limitations of the celluloid lesbian community.

In addition to the radical, lesbian photography and performance art, *Go Fish* is also indicative of the proximity between experimental, avant-garde and cross-over queer films in the early 1990s. The short scene discussed above is reminiscent of Su Friedrich's short film *First Comes Love* (1991), which intercuts wedding scenes until its conclusion, when a rolling list over the final images names all the countries in which same-sex marriage was illegal in 1991. Films, such as *Go Fish*, *The Watermelon Woman* and *Paris is Burning*, became cross-over successes and thus set the stage for later mainstreaming of gay and lesbian themes and films, while avant-garde and experimental filmmakers, such as Su Friedrich, remained in the art-house circuit.

If queerness does not constitute a clear, demarcated identity, the boundaries of community can also not be defined in absolute terms. In one scene in *Go Fish*, without any narrative motivation or introduction, we see Daria having sex with a man in a silent shot that emphasises and aestheticises their bodies. The scene is jarring because it is the only moment a male character appears in the film. We then see Daria walking through the night alone, being pulled away by two leather-clad women. One expects homophobic violence common in gay films when characters walk alone at night (see for example Kutlug Ataman's *Lola + Bilidikid* (*Lola and Billy the*

Kid) (1999), *Looking for Langston*, *The Living End*). Rather, members of the dyke community surround Daria and aggressively question and confront her about having sex with a man while claiming to be a lesbian. Instead of an indictment or validation of her behaviour, we encounter different attitudes. The film itself does not endorse a singular position, but the staging of the circle and the aggressive attacks against Daria offer her as a figure for audience identification. The film thus undermines claims to lesbian authenticity, which goes along with the film's emphasis on style: the characters are queer because every day they make themselves over through self-stylisation and negotiation with other members of the community. The film neither endorses prescriptive definitions for lesbian identity, nor a policing of boundaries for a queer community.

This independent film radically reconfigures the love story, a genre fraught with heterosexual conventions. Instead of love at first sight, Max and Ely are brought together by the community, in which they and their story are embedded. When Max and Ely finally get together, instead of romance, the film continues its emphasis on the mundane every-day. The film also does not follow the cinematic conventions of romance with soft focus, lighting and music. Heavy breathing accompanies their kissing and sex but non-diegetically by several characters, which breaks the realist illusion. After their first date, Max shares its account with Kia and Evy, while Ely shares with Daria. Their stories are accompanied by reenactments of their date; thus viewers get to see the 'first date' three times as it circulates in the community. Audience members are situated as part of that community, since the story addresses them as well. Max and Ely's love story becomes a narrative thread that ties the community together.

The Watermelon Woman addresses the serious political issues of the invisibility of black lesbians in film history, in a comedy, thus avoiding the emphasis on suffering and despair that characterised earlier films about lesbians. Similar to *Go Fish*, *The Watermelon Woman* includes vignettes that interrupt the narrative without breaking the flow, in part because the entire film is based on a video aesthetic and in part because as a film about filmmaking, these vignettes reflect on the medium itself. By the time she made her first feature film, Dunye was known for her shorts *Janine* (1990), *She Don't Fade* (1991), *Vanilla Sex* (1992), *Untitled Portrait* (1993), *The Potluck and the Passion* (1993) and *Greetings from Africa* (1996), which are all between eight and thirty minutes long independently produced films that address race and lesbian desire from an auto-biographical perspective.

In *The Watermelon Woman*, Dunye plays a young aspiring filmmaker in Philadelphia named Cheryl who works in a video store with her friend Tamara with whom she co-owns a commercial video business that films weddings and community events. Cheryl becomes interested in a black female actress playing 'Mammie' roles in so-called race films, for example *Plantation Memories*. When researching the actress credited as 'the Watermelon Woman', Cheryl discovers that she was a lesbian who seemed to have had a relationship with the film's white director, Martha Page. Cheryl traces the roots of 'the Watermelon Woman' to the community of black lesbians in 1930s Philadelphia. Famous lesbians appear in cameo roles. Playwright Sarah Schulman, poet Cheryl Clarke, theorist Camille Paglia, producer Alexandra Juhasz and musician Toshi Reagon extend community beyond the narrative. Parallel to her investigation of the past, Cheryl falls in love with a white woman, Diana Rowland, played by Guinevere Turner. Diana tries to help Cheryl with her project, but her fetishisation of black-ness makes a meaningful relationship between them impossible, and at the end of the film they separate. The film concludes with a video docu-mentary about 'the Watermelon Woman'. After the credits roll, a statement on the black screen informs the audience: 'Sometimes you have to create your own history. The Watermelon Woman is fiction. Cheryl Dunye, 1996.'

What appears as documentary is a fictionalised account to highlight the absence of documentation of black lesbians in the film industry. *The Watermelon Woman* juxtaposes the cinematic invisibility of lesbians to two other film traditions: one, wedding videos, and, two, straight pornography. The film opens with Cheryl and Tamara on the job, filming a Jewish-African-American wedding at Bryn Mawr College. One of Cheryl's and Tamara's con-flicts centres on Tamara's enjoyment of black pornography that she keeps ordering for the store. These two visual traditions contrast to the absence of images of black lesbians in film history that makes it impossible for Cheryl, the character, to trace the history of 'the Watermelon Woman' and leads Cheryl Dunye, the filmmaker, to create a character – 'the Watermelon Woman' – and an imaginary search to highlight the absence. The slippage between director Cheryl Dunye who plays the main character and whose mother plays Cheryl's mother in the film, creates an autobiographical dimension, emphasising the presence and agency of African-American queer directors at that historical moment. In both *The Watermelon Woman* and *Looking for Langston*, the narrative emphasises the search for elusive figures that are invested with a desire for identification.

In one scene, Cheryl sits next to the screen on which 'Plantation Memories' is playing and reenacts the exaggerated performance of 'the Watermelon Woman'. The different levels of reenactment and exaggeration comment on 'blackface', the tradition of black performers to exaggerate the performance of blackness to the degree that it becomes a caricature historically based on minstrel shows. Much of the discourse in Queer Studies saw the exaggeration of gender performance in drag queens and camp as a vehicle to deconstruct the assumed naturalness of gender and sexuality. *The Watermelon Woman* emphasises the particularities of raced performance by excavating the violence inherent in the structure of invisibility of lived experience vis-à-vis the hypervisibility of exaggerated performances forced onto the subjects through racist economic structures. It is Cheryl's ability and desire to see through the exaggerated performance of the Mammie role to be able to witness the beauty of 'the Watermelon Woman'. The fictional Watermelon Woman is given an authentic historical context when African-American poet Cheryl Clark in a cameo as 'the Watermelon Woman's' past lover refers to 'all of us stone butches', referencing the history of the unrepresented diversity of black female sexuality.

Despite the international critical and audience success of these films in the early 1990s, New Queer Cinema's directors Dunye, Julien and Parmar lost their funding sources for feature-length films in the United States and the UK throughout the 1990s. Others, such as poet Essex Hemphill and filmmakers Marlon Riggs and Derek Jarman, died of AIDS between 1994 and 1995. Isaac Julien has moved into installation art and documentaries. Cheryl Dunye has completed two feature-length films, one for HBO, *Stranger Inside* (2001) a drama about women in prison, and one studio production, *My Baby's Daddy* (2004), neither of which matched the critical success of *The Watermelon Woman*.

New Queer Cinema, as this chapter has discussed, had an enormous impact on queer cinema, in part because of its thorough engagement with film history and aesthetics, and in part because of its connection to political and artistic movements beyond film. These films received scholarly attention and are tied to the foundation of Queer Film Studies and spoke to the community of queers. The films' extreme aestheticism and references to film history also specifically spoke to the cinephile lovers of film generally. New Queer Cinema ignored simplistic assumptions about processes of audience identification or enlightenment that undergirded earlier films, which either addressed gays and lesbians offering positive figures of identification or liberal audiences to educate them rationally about homosexuality. Paradoxically, the impact of New Queer Cinema opened the door to the mainstreaming of gay and lesbian cinema, topics and characters even if contemporary mainstream films advance very different politics and aesthetics, as outlined in the next and final chapter.

5   GAY COWBOYS, FABULOUS FEMMES
          AND GLOBAL QUEERS

This final chapter portrays the two dominant developments of contemporary queer cinema: one, mainstreaming, particularly in the US, and two, the global proliferation of queer films. The first and more extensive section describes the mainstreaming of gay and lesbian cinema in films that address a general audience and the use of conventional genres for films geared at gays and lesbians. The chapter's second section surveys the international proliferation of queer cinema during the last decade in a cursory overview of queer international cinema and few select readings of films to illustrate transnational queer cinema's simultaneous engagement with national film traditions and the global vocabulary of queer cinema.

Section one moves through a set of American films that signal important stepping stones in the process of societal acceptance for gays and lesbians. In contrast to New Queer Cinema the films discussed in this chapter include traditional genres, such as melodrama, neo-noir and comedy, particularly romantic comedy. Because films with gays and lesbians are made increasingly by Hollywood studios and because the landscape of independent cinema changed, the films discussed in this chapter rely on larger budgets and reflect increased production value than films discussed in the previous chapters.[1] Stars, known to be straight, can 'play gay' without a stigma being attached to it. Mainstreaming implies that the films intentionally address a 'straight', cross-over audience, and in that process desexualise gay and feminise lesbian characters to render them more acceptable to mainstream audiences.

Particular films, analysed in-depth in this chapter's first part, are important markers on the path to acceptance: from Jonathan Demme's *Philadelphia* (1993), Andy and Lana Wachowski's *Bound* (1996) and Frank Oz's *In & Out* (1997) to Ang Lee's *Brokeback Mountain* (2005). As a result of mainstreaming, homosexual characters and codes also appear in comedies that are not marketed as gay at all, such as Jay Rouch's *Austin Powers: The Spy Who Shagged Me* (1999), Adam McKay's *Talladega Nights: The Ballad of Ricky Bobby* (2006), Peter Cattaneo's *The Full Monty* (1997) and Jonathan Dayton and Valerie Faris's *Little Miss Sunshine* (2006), some of which cite and rewrite camp for a generation unfamiliar with its original context. Films explicitly addressing a gay and lesbian audience have also become more mainstream, illustrated by lesbian films of the twenty-first century that follow the traditional narrative conventions of the love story. Katherine Brooks' *Loving Annabelle* (2006), Pawel Pawlikowski's *My Summer of Love* (2004) and Charles Herman-Wurmfeld's *Kissing Jessica Stein* (2001), are a few examples. The chapter ends with a brief overview of contemporary global queer cinema, which incorporates national film traditions and transnational queer culture, and two exemplary readings of gay and lesbian films from China from the early years of the twenty-first century.

Mainstreaming Gays

On its release in 1993, *Philadelphia* coincided with New Queer Cinema, but addresses itself to a straight, mainstream audience, evident through its narrative, the representation of the main gay character and the casting of avowedly straight Hollywood stars. *Philadelphia* tells the story of Andrew Beckett (Tom Hanks), who is fired by his law firm because he has AIDS and who hires a lawyer to file a wrongful termination law suit against his old employer. His African-American, homophobic lawyer, Joe Miller (Denzel Washington), models a journey from prejudice to acceptance. At the outset Joe Miller is afraid to shake Andrew Beckett's hand for fear that he could contract AIDS. His wife who is more tolerant than him, educates him about homosexuals. Miller's character development allows the film to chart out different positions vis-à-vis homosexuality from ignorance to humanist enlightenment captured by his declaration: 'This is the essence of discrimination!' The film's pedagogical mission consists of debunking stereotypes, teaching viewers that gay men can be black and football players.

The two main characters, Andrew Beckett and Joe Miller, are each associated with one central scene. Taken together, the two moments encapsu-
late the film's politics. Miller symbolises a liberal approach toward non-
discrimination when he delivers a speech about 'our fear of homosexuals'
in the court room, making a rational argument based on a civil rights logic.
As an African-American lawyer, he embodies the rational argument against
discrimination and a legal framework to overcome it. The setting of the
court room in Philadelphia, home of the American constitution, symboli-
cally endorses this logic that underlies a liberal approach toward integration of minorities.

The film uses race to imply a parallel argument about racial and sexual
discrimination. Joe Miller, with his all-American name, signals the endpoint of a process of overcoming institutionalised racism. The implied
parallel structure of African-American and gay discrimination embedded
in legal discourse and rational speech makes for a persuasive rhetorical
strategy but glosses over the different forms racism and homophobia take
in the US. Miller as homophobic identification figure allows audiences to
follow a process toward acceptance that relies on the stereotype of African-
Americans' proclivity toward homophobia and thus implies a homophobic,
and not gay, audience.

The central scene associated with Beckett occurs when he explains his
homosexuality to Miller, talking over diegetic sound of the opera diva and
gay icon Maria Callas. The camera shows Beckett with a skewed angle and
Miller in a straight-on shot. Bathed in red, the scene takes on a surreal
quality that does not aestheticise but denounces queerness's claim to the
sublime beauty of Callas. This portrayal of gay culture as abject mirrors the
film's relationship to the gay body marked by lesions. Similarly, the depiction of the long-term gay relationship without visible physical interaction
between Beckett and his lover Miguel Alvarez (Antonio Banderas) anticipates
a possible homophobic response toward an explicit representation of gay
sexuality. These two scenes illustrate how the film associates heterosexual
masculinity with rationality and the legal discourse of citizenship in contrast
to connecting homosexuality with an abject body reduced to a desire for the
disembodied sublime beauty of Maria Callas.

While these are the ways in which *Philadelphia* partakes in the mainstreaming of homosexuality, the film also connects to New Queer Cinema.
Mainstream and subversion are not mutually exclusive but co-depending,

shifting and changing circumscriptions. In addition to the avowedly heterosexual Hollywood stars cast in the main roles, actresses and actors in
minor roles point to a queer community that participated in the making
of the film. Karen Finley, mentioned as one of the NEH 4 in the previous
chapter, plays Dr Gillman. Also connected to a queer network is Ron
Vawter, who appeared in *Born in Flames* (see chapter three), *Swoon* and
Shu Lea Cheang's *Fresh Kill* (1994), and during the early 1990s toured with
a performance entitled 'Roy Cohn/Jack Smith', investigating the dyad of
homosexuality and homophobia, made into a film, *Roy Cohn/Jack Smith*
(1994). Vawter died of a heart attack in 1994, presumably related to the fact
that he had contracted AIDS. His screen presence therefore encapsulates
the continuing complexity of visibility/invisibility of homosexuality. In a
tragic irony, in a film about homosexuality and AIDS, the hypervisibility
of the avowedly straight stars marginalises the gay actor except for those
viewers familiar with queer culture.

While *Philadelphia* inscribed homosexuality as suffering maleness
in the age of AIDS but advocated a liberal and rational discourse of
anti-discrimination, another dimension of mainstreaming commodified
lesbian sexuality and turned it into an expression of style. Three years
after *Philadelphia*, Andy and Larry Lana Wachowski, later directors of
cult-classic *The Matrix* (1999) and its sequels, co-directed *Bound*, which
mainstreamed the roles of butch and femme. In this neo-noir film, a genre
with exaggerated film-noir conventions, a butch/femme couple takes
on the Mafia. The Wachowski siblings exaggerate the genre traits of the
violence and eroticisation, reflecting their interest in cyberpunk, comics
and animation. Femme Violet (Jennifer Tilly), the girlfriend of a gangster
Caesar (Joe Pantoliano), has a steamy affair with her neighbour, the butch
lesbian Corky (Gina Gershon). The film opens with Corky bound in a closet
– a loaded metaphor in this context – and continues mounting suspense
whether the two women can outsmart the mob, steal Caesar's money and
escape his hyper-violence until the happy ending.

Bound lifts signifiers of lesbian identity into the mainstream. Black
leather outfits that both women wear, Corky's tattoo of a double ax, the
truck she drives and her men's underwear move from subcultural signs
of lesbian recognition to becoming fashion statements. Feminist lesbians
interpreted the double ax, the labrys, used in ancient Knossos on Crete in
religious ceremonies conducted by Minoan priestesses, as a symbol for lost

Andy and Lana Wachowski's *Bound* (1995)

matriarchy. It functioned as a sign of recognition among lesbians, especially during the 1970s and 1980s. Similarly, tattoos once belonged to alternative subcultures of prisoners, sailors, bikers and 'primitive' societies. Now they evoke this history of marginalisation without belonging to it.

Butch and Femme Go Mainstream

Marking the development from subcultural signifiers to features of mainstream entertainment, accoutrements of lesbianism can now be taken on or off like fashion accessories. For example, in the opening of McG's [Joseph McGinty Nichol] *Charlie's Angels* (2000), Cameron Diaz as Natalie, one of the three 'angels', performs in what became a famous dance scene in Fruit of the Loom Marvel Heroes boys' underwear: detached from sexual politics, cross-dressing now spells cute. The commodification of these signifiers relies on their ability to evoke transgression without subverting gender or sexual norms.

Bound manages to speak to both mainstream audiences through the conventions of genre cinema and the sexualisation of the female characters and to queer audiences by siding with the lesbian couple that overcomes the mob. When Caesar asks Corky what she did to Violet, she answers: 'Everything you couldn't do.' The film's over-the-top-sexualisation and hyperbolic stereotypes approximates camp, bringing lesbians out of the closet in a flamboyant way and offering the viewing pleasure of a queer fantasy. The female characters' stylish sex-appeal contrasts to earlier images of lesbians either as desexualised and suffering or imbued with a monstrous and destructive sexuality. The exchange of erotic desire between the two women transgresses Caesar's heterosexual 'ownership' of Violet.

Yet Corky's butchness in her role as a handywoman with men's underwear, short haircut and tattoo can become visible on screen only because underneath it all, the white, slender actress adheres to the beauty standards that makes her sexual attraction palatable for an audience accustomed to Hollywood stars. After Corky came out of closet and drove into the sunset with her femme, the butch lesbian has left the set and now rarely reappears in mainstream cinema, populated by long-haired, well-dressed femmes, the so-called lip-stick lesbians who emerged in the late 1990s. The figure of the butch not only signifies a non-normative desire but also bends gender in her appropriation of masculine signifiers, and thus represents more of a threat toward heterosexuality than the figure of the femme. It is no surprise then that mainstream films and television series embraced white femmes, from *Friends* to *The L-Word*, while independent documentaries gave voice to black butches, for example Debra A. Wilson's *Butch Mystique* (2003) and Daniel Peddle's *The Aggressives* (2005).

The process of mainstreaming relies on genre cinema. In contrast to New Queer Cinema, films with gay and lesbian themes around the turn of the twenty-first century increasingly adhered to the narrative conventions of genres familiar to audiences. Historically, genre had been coded according to gender; western and gangster films address a heterosexual, male audience; the melodrama and romance are geared toward heterosexual women; and the musical is considered to be gay.[2] Late in the 1990s, Franz Oz's *In and Out* pokes fun at the genre of the socially-conscious liberal drama. Only four years after *Philadelphia*, *In and Out* indicates the sea change that gay and lesbian representation had undergone throughout the 1990s.

In and Out's main character, Howard Brackett, fictionalises the teacher outed by Tom Hanks in his 1994 Academy Award acceptance speech for his role in *Philadelphia*, when he thanked his gay high school drama teacher. Despite Brackett exhibiting all kinds of gay stereotypes, he lives a regular straight life in small-town America until he is outed in an Academy Award acceptance speech. The comedy relies on an audience's familiarity with gay codes, for example the love for Barbra Streisand, to which Brackett, however, is blind. *In and Out* also plays with stereotypes of gay effeminacy and straight masculinity when it casts Tom Selleck, long-time main character of the American action television series *Magnum PI* (1980–88) and outspoken conservative, as a gay reporter who falls in love with Brackett.

The jokes pivot on 'the closet', the figure that captures the simultaneity of invisibility and visibility. In the final scene, Brackett announces that he is gay in the high school auditorium, and individual audience members stand up and also declare their homosexuality, following the conventions of liberal films that create the triumphant collective solidarity with the individual who has overcome the odds. The closet has become obsolete when anybody can 'out' themselves at will. The film also playfully rewrites the structure of the gay rumour that becomes self-fulfilling, as in *The Children's Hour*, which ends in suicide and despair, in contrast to *In and Out*'s ironic communal embrace of queerness in Middle America.

Indicators of increasing acceptance are the presence of gays and lesbians as minor characters in comedies, such as Peter Cattaneo's *The Full Monty* (1997), Christopher Guest's *Best in Show* (2000) and Jonathan Dayton's and Valerie Faris's *Little Miss Sunshine*. A comedy targeting twenty-something young, straight, male audience, such as Adam McKay's *Talladega Nights: The Ballad of Ricky Bobby*, can include gay sexual innuendos without fear of losing its intended audience. Addressing a generation that grew up long after Stonewall, a film such as Jay Roach's *Austin Powers: The Spy who Shagged Me* employs former gay codes for a world without the necessity of double talk. Jokes increasingly emerge from the incongruence that coded references to gayness create when homosexuality has become socially acceptable. The early twenty-first century phenomenon of the 'metrosexual' captures this development by referring to urban men who sport refined tastes in clothes, interior design, personal hygiene and foods without being gay. Johnny Depp as Jack Sparrow in Gore Verbinski's *Pirates of the Caribbean: The Curse of the Black Pearl* (2003) could queer the performance of the main character, a pirate, in a film aimed at children without making the character gay or being protested.

The end of the 'closet' enabled a cultural articulation that looks like camp but functions fundamentally different. Gay sensibility made an event, act or artifact readable as camp. The 'gay-acting' straight guy appears in the spoof of James Bond films, *Austin Powers*, in the most unlikely of characters, Dr Evil who spreads his pinky when he drinks his coffee and uses a 'gay' intonation. An analysis of a brief scene in *Austin Powers* set on Dr Evil's island illustrates that this new form of humour looks like, but is not camp. Dr Evil, a combination of evil characters in James Bond films, asks Frau Farbissina [pronounced '*Verbissene*', German for 'a grim woman']: '*Wie geht es Ihnen?*' ['How are you?'] The language marks her as German, her costume and hair as a woman from the 1920s, an early high point of the lesbian rights movement (see chapter one). In the context of James Bond films, her character also evokes Russian counter-intelligence agent Rosa Klebb in Terence Young's early Bond film, *From Russia with Love* (1963). Avant-garde exile German singer and actress Lotte Lenya played Klebb with s/m undertones mobilising the lesbian stereotype of the unattractive, predatory butch. Her portrait of a masculine woman in turn vilified the Russian enemy.

Austin Powers excavates the homophobic coding of Rosa Klebb for a target audience that is not familiar with its historical references, neither of the mobilisation of homophobia in the depictions of female Russian military in the Cold War ideologies of James Bond films, nor the history of exile of Jewish avant-garde artists Lotte Lenya and her husband Kurt Weill and gays and lesbians during the Hitler regime. Frau Farbissina then answers: 'I have come to embrace the love that dare not speak its name. To my right is my lover. We met at the LPGA [Ladies Professional Golf Association] Tour. Her name is Unibrou.' Her announcement cites from an archive of queer culture: Weimar lesbian subculture, Oscar Wilde's coded definition of homosexual love, the women-only parties and rumours about lesbian players surrounding the LPGA Tour, and resistance to Western female beauty standards, as in the painterly eyebrows in the self-portraits by famous bisexual painter Frieda Kahlo. Wilde captures homosexuality through the paradox of not naming it. But since Frau Farbissina and Unibrou are 'out', this description of homosexuality does not make sense anymore and turns into an incongruous performance by Frau Farbissina. Here we encounter postmodern pastiche that does not add up to a political stance about the current moment, except to point out that references to lesbian community and politics are residues of outdated dogmatism.

A preliminary culmination of the process of mainstreaming is Ang Lee's *Brokeback Mountain*, a more serious gay film. Lee's highly successful film intervened in a public discourse about the self-understanding of the American nation and masculinity by rewriting the conventions of the western, the unreconstructed, heterosexually masculine genre born out of the open space of the American West. It symbolises the normal presence of gays and lesbians in Hollywood but more importantly revises the link between genre and gender by imploding the western through the conventions of the domestic melodrama. Film critics applauded the film because it 'brought a gay couple to the forefront of US genre cinema', 'achieved a breakthrough' and 'resonated with audiences', continuing Lee's early contributions to gay and lesbian cinema with *Xi Yan* (*The Wedding Banquet*) (1993) (White 2007: 20).

Brokeback Mountain begins in 1963 in Signal, Wyoming. Jack Twist, a rodeo rider, and Ennis Del Mar, a ranch hand, meet herding sheep together in the summer, and, unexpectedly for both, fall in love with each other. Unable to create a life together, they go their separate ways, each get married, and engage in secret double lives through irregular trips they take together. Ennis's wife divorces him after she sees the two men kissing. Jack is killed in a hate crime covered up by those around him, and the film ends with Ennis alone with his memories of their deep, yet publicly unacknowledged love.

Brokeback Mountain follows the genre conventions of the western with long takes of wide shots that show the open spaces of wild nature, accompanied by a sound of a single guitar track. Ennis and Jack are cowboys – 'authentic American heroes, self-reliant and brave, honorable and loyal' – who communicate in minimalist dialogue often with their hats pulled deep over their faces, making them inscrutable (see Kitses 2007: 24). The genre creates a dialectic relationship between the excessive vast exteriority and inaccessible masculine interiority, endowing the landscape to communicate what characters can neither allow themselves to feel, nor are able to express.

Lee subverts the western through the conventions of the domestic melodrama. On Brokeback Mountain one of the men is responsible for food and the other for the sheep, which mimics a traditionally gendered division of labour. One day, when Jack arrives from herding sheep and dinner is not ready, he accuses Ennis: 'I'm with the sheep all day and hungry and come down here and there is nothing but beans.' In the western 'direct action' moves in linear fashion, while in the domestic melodrama 'the social pressures' limit 'the range of "strong" actions' (Elsaesser 1991: 56, 79). When Ennis leaves Jack at the end of the summer he does not say anything to him but breaks down in a barn to cry. The scene captures his inability to overcome the social conventions and acknowledge his gay feelings.

Brokeback Mountain captures the internalised and externalised violence associated with masculinist socialisation and heterosexist institutions. Ennis and Jack's conflict circles around Ennis's belief that he cannot overcome societal norms: 'There's nothing we can do. I'm stuck with what I got here.' In the domestic or family melodrama the 'world is closed, and the characters are acted upon. Melodrama confers on them a negative identity through suffering' (Elsaesser 1991: 79). In their rare conversations, they cast their emotions in tragic terms of impossibility and despair. To Jack's 'Sometimes I miss you so much, I can hardly stand it', Ennis responds: 'I wish I knew how to quit you.' Jack dreams that they could live together on a ranch but in a key scene Ennis recounts his childhood memory of two men who 'ranched together', one of whom was later found tortured to death. His father made sure that he and his brother saw this to internalise the threat of punishment for transgressing the prohibition of sexual and emotional relations between men. Tragically, the two characters repeatedly deny each other's love because they see no future so that the narrative development remains circular until external violence ends their cycle of mutual attraction and rejection.

If, as Thomas Elsaesser claims, 'melodrama is iconographically fixed by the claustrophobic atmosphere of the bourgeois home and/or the small-town setting', then Lee manages to show how homophobia turns the lovers' world into a claustrophobic universe despite the wide-open spaces that are the film's primary setting (1991: 84). Nature becomes associated with the characters' sexual freedom and emotional intimacy, while their domestic lives are increasingly associated with repression. The film shows the violence inherent in ideologies of manliness but at the same time cannot escape the attraction that the figure of the lone cowboy holds for a fantasy of autonomy, here recalibrated as the hope for an alternative life at the horizon of the vast landscape. Despite its great achievement, the film's genre-based investment in vast space as a sublime site for autonomous self-realisation and the abjection of the domestic setting as the site of repression, here of gay desire, turns the wives into prime ventriloquists of society's homophobia.

In summary, mainstreaming reflects larger cultural processes of acceptance and normalisation of gays and lesbians. Buried underneath the liberal politics of gay visibility, such films as *Philadelphia* and *Brokeback Mountain*, rely on the feminine as abject to advance a positive discourse about homosexual rights. Mainstream films integrate gay and lesbian characters in genres, such as the western, comedy and romance, include stars cast in main roles and follow conventional aesthetics, such as linear narratives. These films abandon political critiques and in that process desexualise homosexuality and feminise lesbians.

Femme Romance

The inclusion of gay themes and characters in mainstream films parallels the mainstreaming of films targeting gay and lesbian audiences in depoliticised, big budget, genre-based, light entertainment, illustrated here with examples of lesbian romance. Beginning in the 1995, lesbian love stories have come out in the US, Canada and the UK: Maria Maggenti's *The Incredibly True Adventures of Two Girls in Love* (1995), Alex Sichel's *All Over Me* (1997), Anne Wheeler's *Better Than Chocolate* (1999), Charles Hermann-Wurmfeld's *Kissing Jessica Stein*, Alice Wu's *Saving Face* (2004), Pawel Pawlikowski's *My Summer of Love*, Desiree Lim's *Floored by Love* (2005), Katherine Brooks' *Loving Annabelle* (2006), and Jamie Babbit's *Itty Bitty Titty Committee* (2007). The majority of these are light-hearted comedies, often romantic comedies of error, in which a figure from the past motivates confusion until the happy ending ensues with accepting parents, children, friends and ex-lovers.

Several films negotiate immigrant and ethnic communities, most often hinging on traditional parents, such as *Better Than Chocolate*, *Saving Face*, and *Floored by Love*. Sometimes these films show us parents more understanding than their lesbian daughters imagined. In *Kissing Jessica Stein*, the mother endorses the lesbian partner before her daughter mentions her, and in *Itty Bitty Titty Committee*, the main character's mother unexpectedly has lesbian friends and worked at *Ms.* magazine in the past. Few films address interracial lesbian relationships, as does *The Incredibly*

True Adventures of Two Girls in Love or class conflicts, as does *My Summer of Love*. Brooks' *Loving Annabelle* updates the boarding school genre.

These lesbian romances leave behind the feminist critique of patriarchy and its heterosexist institutions, such as marriage. The following two films illustrate the depoliticisation of lesbian cinema: *Kissing Jessica Stein* casts aside earlier tenants of political lesbian film, whereas *Itty Bitty Titty Committee* attempts to return a young generation of lesbians back to politics. In *Kissing Jessica Stein*, Helen, a gallery owner who has multiple affairs with men, looks for a lesbian lover in a personal ad, which Jessica, a straight, single Jewish woman answers because the ad quotes her favorite author, Rainer Maria Rilke. Helen and Jessica become attracted to each other and slowly get involved but have to overcome Jessica's neurotic anxiety about (lesbian) sex. Jessica works for Josh Meyers, whom she dated in college and who is still in love with her. She keeps her new relationship a secret from her colleagues, friends and parents because she does not want to come out as a lesbian before she is sure about her new-found identity. Consequently, Helen feels rejected. The couple overcomes these obstacles only for Helen to break up with Jessica because she is ultimately not sexually satisfied in the relationship. The film ends with Helen in a relationship with another woman, while Jessica, single again, runs into Josh in a bookstore and signals to him that she is available. The final shot shows Jessica and Helen, who are now best friends, in a restaurant sharing Jessica's excitement about Josh.

Narratively, Jessica's lesbian escapade becomes the detour on the road to a heterosexual union, typical for the genre of the romantic comedy, particularly in its incarnation as the 'chick flick', in which a single woman in the big city cannot find a man until coincidence, fate and the happy ending brings them together (see Ferriss and Young 2008). Same-sex desire, reduced to 'kissing' in the film's title, becomes another accessory for women without consequences for their social world or their subjectivity. The figure of the accidental lesbian is not entirely new (see chapter three), but this new breed of the sexual tourist is feminine, likes to accessorise and walks away emotionally unharmed and sexually enriched, in contrast, for example, to Lianna of the film with the same title. The ease, with which Jessica and Helen switch from romance to friendship, encapsulates the superficiality of their relationship. If diamonds once were a girl's best friend, now her best friend is her one-time femme ex-lover.

Seemingly as a reaction to films such as *Kissing Jessica Stein*, *Itty Bitty Titty Committee* responds to the effects of the mainstreaming of lesbianism, its commodification, depoliticisation and the disappearance of its contours by attempting to return the new generation of young lesbians to activism. Latina high-school graduate Anna works in a beauty clinic in Los Angeles that performs breast implants. One night, she encounters rebel Sadie spray-painting the clinic. Sadie invites Anna to a C(i)A (Clits in Action) meeting. The group of young, anarchist, punk, radical-feminist queers around Sadie includes Meat, Shulie and Aggie. The women in their late teens and early twenties represent a range of lesbian, bisexual and transgender women, and embody the characteristics and concerns of third-wave feminism. Anna falls in love with Sadie, who seems unavailable until the very end, and organises C(i)A's biggest protest event, which takes place during a talk show, when the group takes over a TV station and reveals the Washington Monument on national television as a giant penis. Guinevere Turner, who acted in *Go Fish* and *The Watermelon Woman* in the 1990s, plays the established talk show host and provides a bridge to the past of the low-budget aesthetics of New Queer Cinema. *Itty Bitty Titty Committee* is loosely based on the racial-feminist underground classic *Born in Flames*, which relied on a materialist analysis for guerilla activism and tied the movement 'against violence against women' to anti-colonial liberation (see chapter three). Reflecting the shift from second- to third-wave feminism, *Itty Bitty Titty Committee*'s political issues concern beauty standards and cultural, instead of material politics.

While the heroines of *Born in Flames* were women, *Itty Bitty Titty Committee* features and addresses girls, which reflects a larger societal and cultural trend, cinematically initiated with the independent video work of Sadie Benning, for example *Girl Power* (see chapter four). *Itty Bitty Titty Committee* references cultural expressions of what feminist scholar Rebecca Munford defines as part of a 'girl culture' that is a 'far more eclectic and politically grounded phenomenon' than the dominant media acknowledges (2004: 143). Cultural representations of girl power are the band Riot Grrrls and the cultural production of zines, self-published forerunners of such magazines as *Bitch* and *Bust*, contemporary young feminist magazines focusing on popular culture. Scholar Ednie Kaeh Garrison defines 'girl power' as a 'young feminist (sub)cultural movement that combines feminist consciousness and punk aesthetics, politics and style' (2000: 142).

In the film, the group's main political target is the beauty industry, a topic very much at the heart of third-wave feminism, ignited by the publication of journalist Naomi Wolf's *The Beauty Myth: How Images of Beauty Are Used Against Women*, originally in 1991. If, however, the third wave of feminists, according to the definition of academics Leslie Heywood and Jennifer Drake, represents the generation 'whose birth dates fall between 1963 and 1974', then this explains why the portrayal of C(i)A seems out of date: at the beginning of the twenty-first century those third wavers would be in their early thirties and forties, the age of the directors, producers and writers of the film, not finishing high school as does the film's main character (see Heywood & Drake 1997). Produced by POWER UP, an all-woman non-profit organisation intended to empower women in the film industry, *Itty Bitty Titty Committee* presumably reflects a genuine attempt to reach young women. But its 'do it yourself' aesthetic of spray paint and guerilla activism is too obviously constructed by the Hollywood apparatus of perfection to reflect genuine low budget.

The depiction of Anna's homelife in an inclusive and supportive ethnic family does not support the film's argument for radical, underground feminist activity. Anna's relationship to her Latino family combines open-minded love and acceptance with an emotional investment in familial traditions, such as her sister's wedding. If social institutions, such as the nuclear, heterosexual family, have changed to the degree that young women can identify as lesbians during high school in a family that invites the daughter's female lover to events and proudly describes her partner to future in-laws, then radical feminism does not emerge from every woman's life experience anymore or at least not this young woman's.

The film wants to have its cake and eat it too, simultaneously portraying a normalised lesbian existence and arguing for the necessity of radical queer/feminist activism. Consequently, it makes its case from a historical perspective of women's oppression. Throughout the film, Shula – named after adored second-wave feminist, Shulamith Firestone – dishes up a smorgasbord of historical facts of women's oppression, knowledge that she has acquired in her training in Women's Studies at Smith College. The film accurately portrays that third wavers encountered feminism in college instead of forging it out of their own life experiences. But the film's argument for guerilla activism as a result of institutionalised education is inorganic and belies the history and dynamic of radical feminist-lesbian activism, then or now.

In conclusion, during the first decade of the twenty-first century, gay and lesbian topics have become more visible, acceptable and thus, also financially viable. A generation of queer directors, writers and producers has made their way into Hollywood. Yet industry forces are such that films have to satisfy the common denominator of audiences' tastes. Films targeted at lesbians have increasingly portrayed romance without political undergirding. Even a film, such as *Itty Bitty Titty Committee*, in its failure to recuperate radical politics for a new generation, constitutes a symptom of the problem instead of the solution as which it presents itself. Even a film, such as *Itty Bitty Titty Committee*, in its failure to recuperate radical politics for a new generation, constitutes a symptom of the problem instead of the solution as which it presents itself. In contrast, a film, such as Lisa Cholodenka's *The Kids Are All Right* (2010) indicates the dual nature of the process of mainstreaming on the one hand and the increasing loss of the productivity of the categories of mainstream versus radical, studio versus independent, entertainment versus politics on the other. The film portrays the everyday of a lesbian family, including the two mothers Jules, played by Julianne Moore, and Nic, played by Annette Bening, who have to deal with the changes resulting from Jules's extra-marital affair with a man and their two children's departure to college. The portrait of familial normalcy and a positive outlook politically claim the sphere of domesticity and the existence of a future – a significant change from the backward-looking lesbian narratives of the past.

Global Queer Cinema

Whereas processes of mainstreaming dominated American gay and lesbian cinema, overlapping and asynchronous practices, ranging from low-budget, alternative, underground to mainstream, big-budget production shaped global queer cinema from the 1990s into the twenty-first century. Some films present genre cinema with gay and lesbian characters, such as Angelina Maccarone's Afro-German lesbian screwball comedy *Alles wird gut* (*Everything Will Be Fine*) (1998) or Susanna Edwards' Swedish murder mystery *Keillers Park* (2006). Films also continue the tradition of engaging with gay and lesbian desires in coming-of-age in films, reflecting different national cinematic traditions and set in diverse historical contexts. For example, Hettie Macdonald's *Beautiful Thing* (1996) reflects British social realism in its representation of two working-class teenagers who fall in love. The French film, André Téchiné's *Wild Reeds* (1994), updates the boarding school narrative to have it take place in France during the Algerian war (see also Griffiths 2008 and Rees-Roberts 2008).

International queer auteurs, such as Ferzan Ozpetek, a Turkish filmmaker whose films take place in Italy and Turkey, Pedro Almodóvar in Spain and Monika Treut in Germany, have produced queer *oeuvres* out of work that by now spans almost three decades. Ozpetek, for example, emphasises erotic attractions between different characters, often in queer communities of friends that include a broad spectrum of sexual desires, repeatedly established over the death of a character, as in *Hamam* (*Steam: The Turkish Bath*) (1997), *Le fati ignoranti* (*His Secret Life*) (2001) and *Saturno contro* (*Saturn in Opposition*) (2001).

Global queer cinema is indebted to national cinematic traditions that intersect with a transnational queer culture. This is the case in two examples from China: Yu Li's *Jin nian xia tian* (*Fish and Elephant*) (2001) and Stanley Kwan's *Lan Yu* (2001). Even though gay and lesbian cinema from Asia had already brought forth an extensive list of films, the early twenty-first century saw an explosion of queer cinema from China, Hong Kong, Korea, Japan, Thailand and the Philippines (see Grossman 2000). *Fish and Elephant* and *Lan Yu* rely on sophisticated narratives that include endearing characters that are neither victims, nor flawless, and realistic representations of China.

Fish and Elephant tells the story of the lesbian relationship between Xiaoqun and Xiaoling. Xiaoqun's mother tries to get her daughter married but Xiaoqun informs men on her dates that she is a lesbian. She then meets Xiaoling at her store where she sells the clothes that she sews. Xiaoling separates from her boyfriend and moves in with Xiaoqun. Meanwhile Wujunjun, Xiaoqun's ex-girlfriend, on the run from the police for the murder of her father, appears at Xiaoqun's workplace at the zoo where Xiaoqun works as a caretaker of an elephant. When Xiaoqun's mother visits unexpectedly, Xiaoqun and Xiaoling hide the fact that they are a lesbian couple. One day Xiaoling sees Xiaoqun with Wujunjun at the zoo together and leaves Xiaoqun, who becomes distraught. Meanwhile, her mother falls in love with a man and shares with her daughter that she will marry him. Xiaoqun reveals to her mother that she is a lesbian. After a period of confusion, her mother accepts her. The end cross-cuts Xiaoling and Xiaoqun making up and making out, with Wujunjun being killed in a shootout with the police, while Xiaoqun's mother is getting married.

Cinematographically the film purports to tell a simple tale by relying on static, medium-long-shots without close-ups. The film emphasises few settings, such as Xiaoqun's room with her bed and her fish tank, a small room next to the elephant house, and Xiaoling's store. *Fish and Elephant* introduces characters in the midst of their mundane everyday activities as caretaker of an elephant and as seamstress. But the film becomes increasingly complex, revealing traumas that underlie the characters' actions. Instead of a focus on individualised emotion, as in classic melodrama of the West, we encounter a network that connects characters with each other. Symbolic acts substitute for close-ups as a supposed reflection of character's interiority. For example, after Xiaoling see Xiaoqun and Wujunjun together, she kills Xiaoqun's fish. The characters express trauma or deep emotion, such as love or despair, in symbolic and transgressive acts.

The two very different films, *Fish and Elephant* and *Lan Yu*, share that the gay and lesbian identity itself is not the problem that motivates the narrative. *Lan Yu*, also set in Beijing, China, covers a longer period, has higher production value, and is set in a more affluent class. Handong Chen, a rich owner of a firm, is introduced to young Lan Yu with whom he develops a relationship. He buys him gifts and gives him money, but also has other young male lovers. Lan Yu, a poor architecture student from the country, sees Handong with his other young lover and leaves him. When Handong receives unofficial warning about up-coming violence on Tiananmen square, he searches for Lan Yu, and they get back together, with Handong giving Lan Yu a car and a lavish house. Soon thereafter Handong marries his female translator because he believes he should enter a traditional heterosexual marriage and have a child, but a year later they divorce. He runs into Yan Lu again and gives him a passport and money to emigrate to the US to study architecture. When Handong is imprisoned for fraud, Lan Yu uses his savings to get him out of prison. They celebrate together with family and friends, but unexpectedly on the next day, Lan Yu dies on a construction site. His death elucidates the recurring voiceover, in which Handong declares his undying love for Lan Yu, revealing the film to be retroactively told by Handong after Lan Yu's death.

The film complicates the presumed association of homosexuality with urbanity, modernism and a lack of tradition, roots and morality. Lan Yu develops from a naïve country bumpkin into a sophisticated urbanite. Handong presents a flawed character, corrupted by money, who assumes that he can buy young men's affection, not understanding Lan Yu's love until it is too late, following the formula of a tragedy. Handong combines destructive traditionalism and ruthless capitalism, whereas Lan Yu embodies deeper values and true emotions, which he does not commodify. Handong wants a traditional family, but lacks a moral framework. The film critiques not only the commodification of sexuality but also of interpersonal relations.

These two films illustrate the diversity within the Chinese national film culture and within global queer cinema in regard to budget and filmic techniques. They share an unapologetic representation of gay and lesbian identity in the negotiation of the pressures of tradition through expectations of kinship. In the context of different national cinematic traditions and a transnational exploration of queer cinema, the self-confident representation of homosexuality constitutes their common denominator.

The most important intervention in recent years has come from Thai director Apichatpong Weerasethakul, whose mysterious and celebrated films *Sud sanaeha* (*Blissfully Yours*) (2002), *Sud pralad* (*Tropical Malady*) (2004), *Sang Sattawat* (*Syndromes and a Century*) (2006) and *Loong Boonmee raleuk chat* (*Uncle Boonmee Who Can Recall His Past Lives*) (2010), which won the Palme d'Or, and the installation *The Primitive* (2009), in instances include gay characters and narratives, but do not adhere to overarching positivist gay politics. Instead, Weerasethakul reworks the conventions of art cinema from the perspective of temporal simultaneity of Thai Bhuddhism and East Asian rapid globalisation, which constitute the time and space of his films' narratives. Referring to the gay couple in *Tropical Malady*, Seung-hoon Jeong asks: 'Does his gay romance have any political nuance of New Queer Cinema?' (2011: 141). According to Jeong, the filmic narrative about the gay couple rejects expectations of 'romantic progression' and a 'modernist journey'; instead, the film shows a 'dispersed urban space with multilayered temporality' and 'the postmodern synchronicity of non-synchronous times', implying the simultaneity of previously thought to be distinct historical developments, such as regional religious traditions and global fashions, cultures and consumption (ibid.). Weerasethakul's films thus neither claim Western-style sexual identity, nor confront those constructs with alternative pre-modern alternatives, but instead reflect on the cinematic possibilities of articulating desire and temporality in the contemporary world.

In conclusion, this last chapter has discussed the developments of contemporary queer cinema. The intense global proliferation has brought forth divergent trends that constitute productive tensions in queer cinema. On the one hand, the last decade witnessed mainstreaming, particularly in Hollywood, which proliferates and normalises gay and lesbian characters and themes, moving from the socially-conscious liberal drama that speaks on behalf of homosexuals to genre cinema, such as comedies and the western. On the other hand, international queer cinema proliferates in diverse ways that exceed an all-encompassing description. The examples of Chinese films, however, illustrate two important aspects of global queer cinema. One, it features self-confident queer characters who do not suffer because they are gay. Two, it simultaneously negotiates national cultural traditions and transnational queer film conventions. Processes of mainstream appropriations and radical politics of representation continue to shape queer cinema as it continues to evolve in unforeseen and productive ways.

CONCLUSION: BOYS WILL BE GIRLS AND GIRLS WILL BE BOYS

From the late twentieth century into the twenty-first, queer visual representation proliferated in unprecedented ways in film, but also on television,
and in emerging new media. Queer film increasingly includes cross-dressing, transgender, transsexual and intersex subjects as characters that
determine narratives in independent and mainstream films, and this, in a
global queer context. The twin development of new media, often seen as
one of the major factors in globalisation, and the deconstruction of gender,
is not coincidental, as digital networks allow both for disembodiment and
alternative forms of embodiment in cyberspace. With the mainstreaming of
gay and lesbian figures at the beginning of the twenty-first century, white,
upper-middle-class gays and lesbians returned as the clean-scrubbed
image of successful and well-adjusted individuals. This development is
most pronounced in American television series, such as *Ellen*, *Friends*,
Will & Grace, *Queer Eye for the Straight Guy* and *The L-Word*, and the
Canadian *Queer as Folk*. These television series indicate a renewed racial
and gendered visual segregation, with African-American men appearing in
the American television series *Noah's Arc*, while the successful American
show, *The L-Word*, is primarily inhabited by white, upper-class and professional femmes.

   The circulation of these mainstreamed images function in an all-media
environment of private gay and lesbian television channels in the United
States, Australia and Germany, for example, but also interfacing multi-
media platforms, in which television series extend to webpages, blogs,

YouTube and DVDs. The mediated texts, images and narratives circulate globally with immediacy. Thus, a backlash against homosexuality, as in proposed anti-gay laws in Uganda or homophobic attacks against the Sarajevo Queer Film Festival, can circulate on global social and political networking sites and enable a transnational response.

While 'celesbians' mark the possibility of being a mainstream star and a lesbian, the global understanding of queer has expanded to include notions of cross-dressing, transgender, transsexual and intersex subjects as characters that often work against established narrative traditions of gay and lesbian film or television series. Kimberly Pierce's *Boys Don't Cry* (1999) famously fictionalises the hate crime against transgender Brandon Teena. John Cameron Mitchell's *Hedwig and the Angry Inch* (2001) is a glam-rock opera organised around a cross-dresser. American independent film by Duncan Tucker, *Transamerica* (2005) allegorises transgender transformation with a road trip through the American heartland.

Films expand the notion of queer in the transnational context, reflecting the broad experience of global transsexuals and transgender subjects in diverse filmic traditions. Lucia Puenzo's haunting *XXY* (2007), set in a remote fishing village in Argentina, tells the story of an intersex teenager raised female with the help of hormones until she has to decide which gender to take on by either continuing with drug therapy or undergoing a sex-assignment operation. The process of the decision is marred by a visit of a family with a boy who falls in love with her and her inability to reciprocate because of her conflicted relationship to her own body. The film confronts questions of biology, culture and self-determination through scenes of operations on turtles that her father rescues. Ekachai Uekrongtham's *Beautiful Boxer* (2004) depicts the real-life story of transsexual Asanee Suwan, born poor in the Thai countryside, who takes up Thai-boxing to save money for a sex-reassignment operation. Films, such as Pedro Almodovar's *La mala educación* (*Bad Education*) (2004) and Pernille Fischer Christensen's *En Soap* (*A Soap*) (2006) situate cross-dressing in the different national contexts of catholic education in Spain on the one hand and the supposedly tolerant Sweden on the other. Alain Berliner's *Ma vie en rose* (*My Life in Pink*) (1997) offers an endearing portrait of a suburban family trying to come to terms with their boy's desire to dress in girl's clothes, while Kutlug Ataman's *Lola and Billy the Kid* presents gritty urban realism of a group of Turkish gay men who form a cross-dressing belly dancing group (see Mennel 2004 and 2008).

For some films, the political concern is the oppression of the two-gender system; for others cross-dressing becomes a metaphor to negotiate political border crossings in a globalised world. Angelina Maccarone's *Fremde Haut* (*Unveiled*) (2005) portrays an Iranian woman who cannot receive political asylum in Germany for being persecuted as a lesbian in Iran; she consequently takes on the role of a fellow Iranian man who killed himself. In Neil Jordan's *The Crying Game* (1992) and his *Breakfast on Pluto* (2005) cross-dressing is entangled with the politics of Ireland vis-à-vis the UK. Stephan Elliott's *The Adventures of Priscilla, Queen of the Desert* (1994) connects cross-dressing adventures to indigenous rights in Australia.

The cinematic preoccupation with different configurations of lived bodies and embodied desires in their many sexed and gendered variations continues to proliferate, particularly in independent queer cinema. Recent films engage with topics that, in as-of-yet scholarly unexplored ways, echo Magnus Hirschfeld's collection of diverse embodiments of sexuality and gender archived in his series of photographs of cross-dressers, transvestites and members of the so-called 'third sex' in the early twentieth century. The contemporary films do not intend to create such ethnographies but engage anew the lived experiences of transgender youth, as well as intersexuality and asexuality. For example, based on the conventions of cinematic realism, Céline Sciamma's *Tomboy* (2011) from France offers a sensitive portrayal of a child passing as a boy in the neighborhood in conflict with the parents' view of the main character as gendered female. Australian Phoebe Hart's *Orchids: My Intersex Adventure* (2010) and American J. B. Ghuman, Jr.'s *Spork* (2010) present two formally juxtaposed explorations of intersexuality. Whereas the former relies on the tradition of the autobiographical documentary to trace the relations of intersexed interviewees to their own bodies, the latter appropriates the conventions of 1980s high school dramas for a musical comedy about an intersexed teenager. Finally, Angela Tucker's *(A)sexual* (2011) documents people who consciously choose not to be sexually active.

The continuation of genre traditions, such as the documentary format and the realist drama, as well as the appropriation of musical comedies evocative of the 1980s, break assumed correlations between identity politics and realism vis-a-vis queer subversion and camp. Parallel to re-imagining multiple permutations of sex, gender and desire, directors have severed the link between political position and film form. These kinds of films confront the question of biology relying on queer and feminist theory without being bound by its paradigms. While the New Queer Cinema of the 1990s mirrored queer theory's deconstruction of the sex/gender system, which in turn had been introduced by feminism in the 1970s, these films of the second decade of the twenty-first century approach the questions produced by non-normative bodies and desires without a prior ideology projected onto the representation of sexuality and gender. Hence, they redefine queer cinema and traverse its territory with humour and sensitivity, realism and artifice, mainstream address and camp subversion, documentary convention and realist form.

The films discussed in this conclusion lay bare the relationship among gender, sexual identity and desire as more complex than an alignment of biological sex, social gender and innate desire promises. sexual identity and desire as more complex than an alignment of biological sex, social gender and innate desire promises. Global films about transgender, intersex and cross-dressing leave behind the assumed correlation among coherent gender identity, sexual desire and linear narrative. The expansion of queer to include a deconstruction of gender and sexuality and use of new technology comes together in such multi-media art works. Shu Lea Cheang's web-based project 'Brandon' (1998–99), inspired by the story of cross-dressing Brandon Teena, and Ataman's multi-media installation 'Women Who Wear Wigs' (1999), which present different women who wear wigs, including a cross-dresser and a cancer survivor, are just two such examples from the late 1990s. These multi-media and web-based projects move beyond the medium of film and allow for renewed engagement with the questions of gender and sexuality, continuing the multiplicity of queer representation begun at the onset of the twentieth century.

NOTES

Chapter 3

1   Feminist activist Anne Koedt attributed the statement to radical feminist Ti-Grace Atkinson as 'Feminism is the theory; lesbianism is the practice' in an 1971 pamphlet distributed by the Chicago Women's Liberation Union entitled 'Lesbianism and Feminism' (reprinted in Koedt 1973). However, according to scholar of radical feminism Barbara A. Crow in her 'Introduction: *Radical Feminism*' this is a 'familiar and misrepresented quote' (2000: 5). Feminist scholar Katie King traces the development of the phrase, which she suggests 'most women in the US women's movement have heard' (1994: 125). The version that circulates most commonly uses the 'copulative' 'and': 'Feminism is the theory, and lesbianism is the practice'. King explains: 'In 1971, Anne Koedt published an essay titled 'Lesbianism and Feminism' in *Notes from the Third Year*, using this phrase as an epigraph', however, in this case with a 'compounding semicolon' (ibid.). Koedt's essay is prefaced by five epigraphs, one reading as: 'Feminism is the theory; lesbianism is the practice – attributed to Ti-Grace Atkinson' (1973: 246). King explains: 'But Atkinson apparently did not use the phrase this way herself. Instead, it dates from a 1970 talk to the New York Chapter of Daughters of Bilitis (DOB), in which she asserted that lesbians and feminists were different groups, groups that perhaps could not work together at all. She said, 'Feminism is a theory; but Lesbianism is a practice'. Not 'the' but 'a'; not connected with 'and' but distinguished by 'but'. The value is on 'theory' here, as politically transformatory, not on 'practice', which is enacted without revolutionary reflection' (1994: 125). This development of a supposed quote, which was never uttered, shows that the question of the relationship between feminism and lesbianism was debated in theoretical literature as well as in the feminist and lesbian movements. At stake in the different variations is the precise relationship between feminism and lesbianism, which is radically reconfigured through grammatical shifts in the false quote's different incarnations. Ultimately, the 'false memory' of the collective makes lesbianism a lived expression of feminism.

2   In 1981 Mulvey also revised her argument in an article that is less often cited; see Mulvey

1988b. For a discussion of the 'gaze' in the context of feminism, film and imperialism, see Kaplan 1997. For an important film that addresses the particular restriction of Black women to become the spectacle in the Hollywood studio system under segregation, see Julie Dash's *Illusions* (1982). For an essay that thinks through the film's theoretical implications regarding gender and race in the politics of filmic representation, see Hartman & Griffin 1991.

Chapter 5

1   For an overview of the development of an industry of indie films in the US focusing on the significance of the Sundance Film Festival and Miramax production company throughout the 1990s, see Peter Biskind's *Down and Dirty Pictures: Miramax, Sundance, and the Rise of Independent Film* (2004), which tells the story of the 1990s in contrast to the 1970s. The effects of the politics of production can be seen a decade later in the production value of independent films. For the context of this book, the key role that gay and lesbian films played in the reshaping of the independent film landscape of the US is important. In 1991, Sundance saw a 'sweep for cutting-edge gay films', and '*Poison* marked a watershed for the festival' (2004: 106). And finally, *The Crying Game*, and the media hype created around 'the secret' by Harvey Weinstein, one half of Miramax, 'was the hit that the Weinsteins had been praying for' according to Biskind (2004: 145). According to Biskind, in 1994, *Go Fish* sold to Goldwyn for $450,000. He comments: 'The sale of *Go Fish*, while relatively unremarkable in itself, was significant, because it was the first time a commercial transaction had actually occurred while the festival [Sundance] was in progress, and as such it became a marker, inaugurating the era of frenzied bidding that characterised the growth of the acquisitions bubble in the mid-1990s' (2004: 155).

2   The closing scene of Mel Brooks' comedy *Blazing Saddles* (1974) illustrates the film industry's awareness of these connotations and their underlying constructions of masculinity. In an absurd finale on the Warner Bros. studio lot the cast of a western rides onto the set of a musical, whose performers and director are coded as being gay. A fight between cowboys and review dancers ensues, in which the latter are as capable as the former. One pair disappears behind the set in a fistfight and reappears in an embrace walking off the set together. This short interlude encapsulates findings by queer theorists about the sexual and gendered coding of genres, the construction of the relationship of gender and sexuality, and the centrality of violence for the construction of masculinity as an encoding of homosexual desire (see Sedgwick 1985).

FILMOGRAPHY

Adventures of Priscilla, Queen of the Desert, The (Stephan Elliott, Australia, 1994)

After Stonewall (John Scagliotti, US, 1999)

Aggressives, The (Daniel Peddle, US, 2005)

Ali Baba and the Forty Thieves (Arthur Lubin, US, 1944)

All Over Me (Alex Sichel, US, 1997)

Alles wird gut (Everything Will Be Fine) (Angelina Maccaroni, Germany, 1998)

Anders als die Anderen (Different from the Others) (Richard Oswald, Germany, 1919)

A Place Called Lovely (Sadie Benning, US, 1991)

Arabian Nights (Jon Hall, US, 1942)

(A)sexual (Angela Tucker, US, 2011)

Aus eines Mannes Mädchenjahren (A Man's Girlhood) (Karl Grune, Germany, 1919)

Austin Powers: The Spy Who Shagged Me (Jay Rouch, US, 1999)

Beautiful Boxer (Ekachai Uekrongtham, Thailand, 2004)

Beautiful Thing (Hettie Macdonald, UK, 1996)

Before Stonewall (Greta Schiller and Robert Rosenberg, US, 1984)

Beggars of Life (William A. Wellman, US, 1928)

Best in Show (Christopher Guest, US, 2000)

Better than Chocolate (Anne Wheeler, Canada, 1999)

Blazing Saddles (Mel Brooks, US, 1974)

Blonde Venus (Josef von Sternberg, US, 1932)

Bonnie and Clyde (Arthur Penn, US, 1967)

Born in Flames (Lizzie Borden, US, 1983)

Bound (Andy and Lana Wachowski, US, 1996)

Boys Don't Cry (Kimberly Pierce, US, 1999)

Breakfast on Pluto (Neil Jordan, UK, Ireland, 2005)

Bride of the Monster (Edward D. Wood, Jr., US, 1955)

Bride Retires, The (no director, France, 1902)

Brokeback Mountain (Ang Lee, US, 2005)

Butch Mystique (Debra A. Wilson, US, 2003)

Casablanca (Michael Curtiz, US, 1942)

Cecil B. Demented (John Waters, US, 2000)

Chained Girls (Joseph P. Mawra, US, 1965)

Charlie's Angels (McG [Joseph McGinty Nichol], US, 2000)

Children's Hour, The (William Wyler, US, 1961)

Cleopatra (Cecil B. DeMille, US, 1934)

Compulsion (Richard Fleischer, US, 1959)

Crying Game, The (Neil Jordan, UK, 1992)

Das Bildnis des Dorian Gray (*The Picture of Dorian Gray*) (Richard Oswald, Germany, 1917)

Das Cabinet des Dr. Caligari (*The Cabinet of Dr. Caligari*) (Robert Wiene, Germany, 1920)

Das Testament des Dr. Mabuse (*The Testament of Dr. Mabuse*) (Fritz Lang, Germany, 1933)

Der blaue Engel (*The Blue Angel*) (Josef von Sternberg, Germany, 1930)

Der Fall des Generalstabs-Oberst Redl (*The Case of Colonel Redl*) (Karl Anton, Germany, 1931)

Der Fürst von Pappenheim (*The Masked Mannequin*) (Richard Eichberg, Germany, 1927)

Der Geiger von Florenz (*Impetuous Youth*) (Paul Czinner, Germany, 1926)

Der Himmel auf Erden (*Heaven on Earth*) (Alred Schirokauer, 1927, Germany)

Desert Hearts (Donna Deitch, US, 1985)

Desperate Living (John Waters, US, 1977)

Die Büchse der Pandora (*Pandora's Box*) (Georg Wilhelm Pabst, Germany, 1929)

Die Jungfrauenmachine (*Virgin Machine*) (Monika Treut, West Germany, 1988)

Doña Juana (Paul Czinner, Germany, 1928)

Dr. Mabuse, der Spieler (*Dr. Mabuse: The Gambler*) (Fritz Lang, Germany,

1922)
Dracula (Tod Browning, US, 1931)
Easy Rider (Dennis Hopper, US, 1969)
Edward II (Derek Jarman, UK, 1991)
Encuentra entre dos Reinas (*Meeting of Two Queens*) (Cecilia Barriga, Spain, 1991)
En Soap (*A Soap*) (Pernille Fischer Christensen, Sweden/Denmark, 2006)
Exzellenz Unterrock (*Excellence Petty-Coat*) (Edgar Klitzsch, Germany, 1921)
Faustrecht der Freiheit (*Fox and his Friends*) (Rainer Werner Fassbinder, West Germany, 1975)
Female Misbehavior (Monika Treut, US, Germany, 1992)
First Comes Love (Su Friedrich, US, 1991)
Flaming Creatures (Jack Smith, US, 1963)
Floored by Love (Desiree Lim, Canada, 2005)
Fox, The (Mark Rydell, US, 1967)
Fresh Kill (Shu Lea Cheang, US, 1994)
From Russia with Love (Terence Young, UK, 1963)
Full Monty, The (Peter Cattaneo, UK, 1997)
Geschlecht in Fesseln (*Sex in Chains*) (William Dieterle, Germany, 1928)
Girl Power (Sadie Benning, US, 1993)
Glen or Glenda (Edward D. Wood, Jr., US, 1953)
Go Fish (Rose Troche, US, 1994)
Graduate, The (Mike Nichols, US, 1967)
Greetings from Africa (Cheryl Dunye, US, 1996)
Hairspray (John Waters, US, 1988)
Hairspray (Adam Schankman, US, 2007)
Hamam (*Steam: The Turkish Bath*) (Ferzan Ozpetek, Italy, Turkey, Spain, 1997)
Hedwig and the Angry Inch (John Cameron Mitchell, US, 2001)
Hours and Times, The (Christopher Münch, US, 1991)
Ich möchte kein Mann sein (*I Don't Want to Be a Man*) (Ernst Lubitsch, Germany, 1918)
Illusions (Julie Dash, US, 1982)
Imitation of Life (Douglas Sirk, US, 1959)
In & Out (Frank Oz, US, 1997)
Incredibly True Adventures of Two Girls in Love, The (Maria Maggenti, US, 1995)

It Wasn't Love (Sadie Benning, US, 1992)
Itty Bitty Titty Committee (Jamie Babbit, US, 2007)
Jack Smith and the Destruction of Atlantis (Mary Jordan, US, 2006)
Janine (Cheryl Dunye, US, 1990)
Jin nian xia tian (*Fish and Elephant*) (Yu Li, China, 2001)
Kids Are All Right, The (Lisa Cholodenka, US, 2010)
Killing of Sister George, The (Robert Aldrich, US, 1968)
Keillers Park (Susanna Edwards, Sweden, 2006)
Kissing Jessica Stein (Charles Herman-Wurmfeld, US, 2001)
Khush (Pratibha Parmar, UK, 1991)
Kustom Kar Kommandos (Kenneth Anger, US, 1965)
La mala educación (*Bad Education*) (Pedro Almodóvar, Spain, 2004)
Le fate ignoranti (*His Secret Life*) (Ferzan Ozpetek, Italy, France, 2001)
Les rendez-vous d'Anna (*The Meetings of Anna*) (Chantal Akerman,
    France, Belgium, West Germany, 1978)
Les roseaux sauvages (*Wild Reeds*) (André Téchiné, France, 1994)
Lianna (John Sayles, US, 1983)
Living End, The (Gregg Araki, US, 1992)
Little Miss Sunshine (Jonathan Dayton and Valerie Faris, US, 2006)
Lan Yu (Stanley Kwan, Hong Kong, China, 2001)
Lola + Bilididikid (*Lola and Billy the Kid*) (Kutlug Ataman, Germany, 1999)
Looking for Langston (Isaac Julien, UK, 1989)
Loong Boonmee raleuk chat (*Uncle Boonmee Who Can Recall His Past
    Lives*) (Apichatpong Weerasethakul, Thailand, UK, France, Germany,
    Spain, Netherlands, 2010)
Loving Annabelle (Katherine Brooks, US, 2006)
Ma vie en rose (*My Life in Pink*) (Alain Berliner, France, Belgium, UK, 1997)
Mädchen in Uniform (*Girls in Uniform*) (Leontine Sagan, Germany, 1931)
Mala Noche (Gus Van Sant, US, 1986)
Maltese Falcon, The (John Huston, US, 1941)
Matrix, The (Andy and Lana Wachowski, US, 1999)
Men of Tomorrow (Leontine Sagan, UK, 1932)
Michael (Carl Theodor Dreyer, Germany, 1924)
Morocco (Josef von Sternberg, US, 1930)
My Baby's Daddy (Cheryl Dunye, US, 2004)
My Beautiful Laundrette (Stephen Frears, UK, 1985)
My Father is Coming (*My Father is Coming*) (Monika Treut, Germany, 1991)

My Own Private Idaho (Gus Van Sant, US, 1991)

My Summer of Love (Pawel Pawlikowski, UK, 2004)

'Necromania': A Tale of Weird Love! (Edward D. Wood, Jr., US, 1971)

Night of the Ghouls (Edward D. Wood, Jr., US, 1959)

Nosferatu (Friedrich Wilhelm Murnau, Germany, 1922)

Orchids: My Intersex Adventure (Phoebe Hart, Australia, 2010)

Outrage (Kirby Dick, US, 2009)

Paris is Burning (Jennie Livingston, US, 1990)

Parting Glances (Bill Sherwood, US, 1986)

Personal Best (Robert Towne, US, 1982)

Philadelphia (Jonathan Demme, US, 1993)

Pirates of the Caribbean: The Curse of the Black Pearl (Gore Verbinski, US, 2003)

Plan 9 from Outer Space (Edward D. Wood, Jr., US, 1959)

Poison (Todd Haynes, US, 1991),

Potluck and the Passion, The (Cheryl Dunye, US, 1993)

Querelle (Rainer Werner Fassbinder, West Germany, 1982)

R.S.V.P. (Laurie Lynd, Canada, 1992)

Rock Hudson's Home Movies (Mark Rappaport, US, 1992)

Rope (Alfred Hitchcock, US, 1948)

Roy Cohn/Jack Smith (Jill Godmilow, US, 1994)

Sang sattawat (*Syndromes and a Century*) (Apichatpong Weerasethakul, Thailand, France, Austria, 2006)

Saturno contro (*Saturn in Opposition*) (Ferzan Ozpetek, Italy, France, Turkey, 2001)

Saving Face (Alice Wu, US, 2004),

Scorpio Rising (Kenneth Anger, US, 1964)

Screen Tests [*Susan, Dennis, Nico, Freddy, Richard, Lou, Jane*] (Andy Warhol, US, 1964–66)

Serial Mom (John Waters, US, 1994)

She Don't Fade (Cheryl Dunye, US, 1991)

She Must Be Seeing Things (Sheila McLaughlin, US, 1987)

Spork (J.B. Ghuman, Jr., US, 2010)

Sud pralad (*Tropical Malady*) (Apichatpong Weerasethakul, Thailand, France, Germany, Italy, 2004)

Sud sanaeha (*Blissfully Yours*) (Apichatpong Weerasethakul, Thailand, France, 2002)

Stranger Inside (Cheryl Dunye, US, 2001)
Suddenly, Last Summer (Joseph L. Mankiewicz, US, 1959)
Swoon (Tom Kalin, US, 1992)
Talladega Nights: The Ballad of Ricky Bobby (Adam McKay, US, 2006)
Ten Commandments, The (Cecil B. DeMille, US, 1956)
Therese and Isabelle (Radley Metzger, US, 1968)
These Three (William Wyler, US, 1936)
Tongues Untied (Marlon Riggs, US, 1989)
Tomboy (Céline Sciamma, France, 2011)
Torch Song (Charles Walters, US, 1953)
Torch Song Trilogy (Paul Borgart, US, 1988)
Totally F***ed Up (Gregg Araki, US, 1993)
Transamerica (Duncan Tucker, US, 2005)
Untitled Portrait (Cheryl Dunye, US, 1993)
Vanilla Sex (Cheryl Dunye, US, 1992)
Verführung: Die grausame Frau (*Seduction: The Cruel Woman*) (Monika
      Treut, West Germany, 1984)
Viktor und Viktoria (*Viktor and Viktoria*) (Reinhold Schünzel, Germany,
      1933)
Watermelon Woman, The (Cheryl Dunye, US, 1996)
Wege zu Kraft und Schönheit (*Ways to Strength and Beauty*) (Nicholas
      Kaufmann and Wilhelm Prager, Germany, 1925)
Wizard of Oz, The (Victor Fleming, US, 1939)
Xi yan (*The Wedding Banquet*) (Ang Lee, Taiwan, US, 1993)
XXY (Lucia Puenzo, Argentina, France, Spain, 2007)
Young Soul Rebels (Isaac Julien, UK, France, Germany, Spain, 1991)

BIBLIOGRAPHY

Andrews, D. (2006) 'Sex Is Dangerous, So Satisfy Your Wife: The Softcore Thriller in Its Contexts', *Cinema Journal*, 45, 3, 59–89.

Babuscio, J. (1999 [1978]) 'The Cinema of Camp (*aka* Camp and the Gay Sensibility)', in F. Cleto (ed.) *Camp: Queer Aesthetics and the Performing Subject: A Reader*. Ann Arbor: The University of Michigan Press, 117–35.

Bad Object Choices (eds) (1991) *How Do I Look?: Queer Film and Video*. Seattle: Bay Press.

Belach, H. and W. Jacobsen (1990) 'Anders als die Anderen (1919): Dokumente einer Kontroverse', in H. Belach and W. Jacobsen (eds) *Richard Oswald: Regisseur und Produzent*. Munich: edition text + kritik, 25–35.

Belton, J. (1996) 'The Production Code', in J. Belton (ed.) *Movies and Mass Culture*. New Brunswick: Rutgers University Press, 135–49.

Benshoff, H. M. (1997) *Monsters in the Closet: Homosexuality and the Horror Film*. Manchester: Manchester University Press.

Biskind, P. (2004) *Down and Dirty Pictures: Miramax, Sundance, and the Rise of Independent Film*. New York: Simon and Schuster.

Bordwell, D. and K. Thompson (2008) *Film Art: An Introduction*. Boston: McGraw Hill.

Brooks, L. (2000 [1974]) *Lulu in Hollywood*. Minneapolis: University of Minnesota Press.

Bunch, C. (2000 [1972]) 'Lesbians in Revolt', in B. A. Crow (ed.) *Radical Feminism: A Documentary Reader*. New York: New York University Press, 332–6.

Butler, A. (1993) '*She Must Be Seeing Things*: An Interview with Sheila

McLaughlin', in M. Gever, J. Greyson and P. Parmar (eds) *Queer Looks: Perspectives on Lesbian and Gay Film and Video*. London: Routledge, 368–76.

Butler, J. (1990) *Gender Trouble: Feminism and the Subversion of Identity*. London: Routledge.

Butler, C. (ed.) (2007) *WACK!: Art and the Feminist Revolution*. Los Angeles: The Museum of Contemporary Art.

Canby, V. (1982) 'Movie Review: *Personal Best* (1982): Olympic Love', *The New York Times* (29 November), n.p. On-line. Available at: http://movies.nytimes.com/movie/review?res=9C07E7DA103BF936A35751C 0A964948260 (accessed 21 July 2012).

Case, S.-E. (1993 [1988]) 'Towards a Butch/Femme Aesthetic' in H. Abelove, M. A. Barale and D. M. Halperin (eds) *The Gay and Lesbian Studies Reader*. London: Routledge, 294–306.

____ (1996) *The Domain-Matrix: Performing Lesbian at the End of Print Culture*. Bloomington: Indiana University Press.

Chauncey, G. (1994) *Gay New York: Gender, Urban Culture, and the Making of the Gay Male World 1890–1940*. New York: Basic Books.

Cleto, F. (ed.) (1999) *Camp: Queer Aesthetics and the Performing Subject: A Reader*. Ann Arbor: The University of Michigan Press.

Comensoli, V. (1993) 'Homophobia and the Regulation of Desire: A Psychoanalytic Reading of Marlowe's *Edward II*', *Journal of the History of Sexuality* 4, 2, 175–200.

Contreras, D. T. (2004) 'New Queer Cinema: Spectacle, Race, Utopia', in M. Aaron (ed.) *New Queer Cinema: A Critical Reader*. Edinburgh: Edinburgh University Press, 119–27.

Corliss, R. (1968) 'Review: *Therese and Isabelle*', *Film Quarterly*, 22, 1, 63–7.

Crow, B. A. (2000) 'Introduction: *Radical Feminism*', in B. A. Crow (ed.) *Radical Feminism: A Documentary Reader*. New York: New York University Press, 1–13.

De Lauretis, T. (1991) 'Film and the Visible', in Bad Object Choices (ed.) *How Do I Look?: Queer Film and Video*. Seattle: Bay Press, 223–64.

____ (2007 [1990]) 'Guerrilla in the Midst: Women's Cinema in the 80s', in J. Stacey and S. Street (eds) *Queer Screen: A Screen Reader*. London: Routledge, 21–40.

Dobler, J. (2003) *Von anderen Ufern: Geschichte der Berliner Lesben und*

Schwulen in Kreuzberg und Friedrichshain. Berlin: Bruno Gmünder Verlag.

Domröse, U. (2008) *Der Fotograf Herbert Tobias (1924–1982): Blicke und Begehren*. Göttingen: Steidl.

Dyer, R. (1990) *Now You See It: Studies on Lesbian and Gay Film*. London: Routledge.

____ (2007) *Pastiche*. London: Routledge.

Ebert, R. (1986) 'Desert Hearts', *Chicago Sun-Times* (6 June), n.p. On-line. Available at: http://rogerebert.suntimes.com/apps/pbcs.dll/article?AID=/19860606/REVIEWS/606060301/1023 (accessed 21 July 2012).

Elsaesser, T. (1991 [1972]) 'Tales of Sound and Fury: Observations on the Family Melodrama', in M. Landy (ed.) *Imitations of Life: A Reader in Film & Television Melodrama*. Detroit: Wayne State University Press, 68–91.

Faderman, L. and B. Eriksson (eds) (1980) *Lesbians in Germany: 1890's–1920's*. Tallahassee: The Naiad Press.

Faderman, L. (1994 [1983]) *Scotch Verdict: Miss Pirie and Miss Woods v. Dame Cumming Gordon*. New York: Columbia University Press.

Ferriss, S. and M. Young (2008) (eds) *Chick Flicks: Contemporary Women at the Movies*. New York: Routledge.

Foucault, M. (1995 [1975]) *Discipline and Punish: The Birth of the Prison*. New York: Random House.

Freud, S. (1995 [1924]) 'The Economic Problem of Masochism', in M. A. Fitzpatrick Hanly (ed.) *Essential Papers on Masochism*. New York: New York University Press, 274–85.

Fuss, D. (1991) *Inside/Out: Lesbian Theories, Gay Theories*. London: Routledge.

Gabilondo, J. (2002) 'Like Blood for Chocolate, Like Queers for Vampires: Border and Global Consumption in Rodríguez, Tarantino, Arau, Esquivel, and Troyano (Notes on Baroque, Camp, Kitsch, and Hybridization)', in A. Cruz-Malavé and M. F. Manalansan IV (eds) *Queer Globalizations: Citizenship and the Afterlife of Colonialism*. New York: New York University Press, 236–63.

Gamman, L. and M. Makinen (1994) *Female Fetishism*. New York: New York University Press.

Garrison, E. K. (2000) 'U.S. Feminism – Grrrl Style! Youth (Sub)Cultures and the Technologics of the Third Wave', *Feminist Studies*, 26, 1, 141–70.

Gever, M., J. Greyson, P. Parmar (eds) (1993) *Queer Looks: Perspectives on Lesbian and Gay Film and Video*. London: Routledge.

Goldsby, J. (1993 [1991]) 'Queens of Language: Paris is Burning', in M. Gever, J. Greyson, P. Parmar (eds) *Queer Looks: Perspectives on Lesbian and Gay Film and Video*. London: Routledge, 108–15.

Gopinath, G. (2002) 'Local Sites/Global Contexts: The Transnational Trajectories of Deepa Mehta's *Fire*', in A. Cruz-Malavé and M. F. Manalansan IV (eds) *Queer Globalizations: Citizenship and the Afterlife of Colonialism*. New York: New York University Press, 149–61.

Grey, R. (1992) *Nightmare of Ecstasy: The Life and Art of Edward D. Wood, Jr.* Portland: Feral House.

Griffiths, R. (ed.) (2008) *Queer Cinema in Europe*. Bristol: Intellect.

Grossman, A. (ed.) (2000) *Queer Asian Cinema: Shadows in the Shade*, *Journal of Homosexuality*, 39, 3–4. New York: The Haworth Place.

Gunning, T. (1990 [1986]) 'The Cinema of Attractions: Early Film, Its Spectator and the Avant Garde', in T. Elsaesser with Adam Barker (eds) *Early Cinema: Space, Frame, Narrative*. London: British Film Institute, 56–62.

Hadleigh, B. (2001 [1993]) *The Lavender Screen: The Gay and Lesbian Films: Their Stars, Makers, Characters & Critics*. New York: Kensington.

Halberstam, J. 'J.' and D. L. Volcano (1999) *The Drag King Book*. London: Serpent's Tail.

Hankin, K. (2002) *The Girls in the Back Room: Looking at the Lesbian Bar*. Minneapolis: University of Minnesota Press.

Hartman, S. V. and F. J. Griffin (1991) 'Are You as Colored as that Negro?: The Politics of Being Seen in Julie Dash's *Illusions*', *Black American Literature* Forum, 25, 2, 361–73.

Heffernan, K. (2004) *Ghouls, Gimmicks, and Gold: Horror Films and the American Movie Business, 1953–1968*. Durham: Duke University Press.

Herzer, M. (2001) *Magnus Hirschfeld: Leben und Werk eines jüdischen, schwulen und sozialistischen Sexologen*. Hamburg: MännerschwarmSkript Verlag.

Heywood, L. and J. Drake (1997) 'Introduction', in L. Heywood and J. Drake (eds) *Third Wave Agenda: Being Feminist, Doing Feminism*. Minneapolis: Minnesota University Press.

Higdon, H. (1999 [1975]) *Leopold & Loeb: The Crime of the Century*. Champaign: University of Illinois Press.

Hoesterey, I. (2001) *Pastiche: Cultural Memory in Art, Film, Literature.* Bloomington: Indiana University Press.

Isenberg, N. (2004) 'Perennial Detour: The Cinema of Edgar G. Ulmer and the Experience of Exile', *Cinema Journal*, 43, 2, 3–25.

Ivory, Y. (2003) 'The Urning and His Own: Individualism and the Fin-de-Siècle Invert', *German Studies Review*, 26, 2, 333–52.

Jameson, F. (1991) *Postmodernism or, The Cultural Logic of Late Capitalism.* Durham: Duke University Press.

Jennings, R. and L. Lominé (2004) 'Nationality and New Queer Cinema: Australian Film', in M. Aaron (ed.) *New Queer Cinema: A Critical Reader.* Edinburgh: Edinburgh University Press, 144–54.

Jeong, Seung-hoon (2011) 'Black Hole in the Sky, Total Exlipse under the Ground: Apichatpong Weerasethakul and the Ontological Turn of Cinema', in K. E. Taylor (ed.) *Dekalog 4: On East Asian Filmmakers,* 140–50.

Kaplan, E. A. (1997) *Looking for the Other: Feminism, Film, and the Imperial Gaze.* London: Routledge.

Kennedy, E. L. and M. D. Davis (1993) *Boots of Leather, Slippers of Gold: The History of a Lesbian Community.* New York: Penguin.

King, K. (1994) *Theory in Its Feminist Travels.* Bloomington: Indiana University Press.

Kitses, J. (2007) 'All that Brokeback Allows', *Film Quarterly*, 60, 3, 22–7.

Knight, J. (1995) 'The Meaning of Treut?', in T. Wilton (ed.) *Immortal, Invisible: Lesbians and the Moving Image.* London: Routledge, 34-51.

Koedt, S. (1973) 'Lesbianism and Feminism' in A. Koedt, E. Levine and A. Rapone (eds) *Radical Feminism.* New York: Quadrangle Books, 246–58.

Kracauer, S. (1974 [1947]) *From Caligari to Hitler: A Psychological History of the German Film.* Princeton: Princeton University Press.

Krafft-Ebing, R. (1965 [1886]) *Psychopathia Sexualis: With Especial Reference to the Antipathic Sexual Instinct.* A Medico-Forensic Study. New York: Arcade.

Kuzniar, A. A. (2000) *The Queer German Cinema.* Stanford: Stanford University Press.

Lamprecht, G. (1968) *Deutsche Stummfilme 1919.* Berlin: Deutsche Kinemathek.

Leidinger, C. (2004) '"Anna Rüling": A Problematic Foremother of Lesbian Herstory', *Journal of the History of Sexuality*, 13, 4, 477–99.

Leung, H. H.-S. (2004) 'New Queer Cinema and Third Cinema', in M. Aaron (ed.) *New Queer Cinema: A Critical Reader*. Edinburgh: Edinburgh University Press, 155–67.

Mann, W. J. (2001) *Behind the Screen: How Gays and Lesbians Shaped Hollywood, 1910–1969*. New York: Viking.

Mennel, B. (1997) '"Germany Is Full of Germans Now": Germanness in Ama Ata Aidoo's *Our Sister Killjoy* and Chantal Akerman's *Meeting with Anna*', in P. Herminghouse and M. Müller (eds) *Gender and Germanness: Cultural Productions of Nation*. Providence, RI: Berghahn, 235–47.

_____ (2004) 'Masochism, Marginality, and Metropolis: Kutlug Ataman's *Lola and Billy the Kid*', *Studies in Twentieth and Twenty-First Century Literature*, 28,1, 289–318.

_____ (2007) *The Representation of Masochism and Queer Desire in Film and Literature*. New York: Palgrave.

_____ (2008) *Cities and Cinema*. London: Routledge.

Mercer, K. (1991) 'Skin Head Sex Thing: Racial Difference and the Homoerotic Imaginary', in Bad Object Choices (ed.) *How Do I Look?: Queer Film and Video*. Seattle: Bay Press, 169–210.

_____ (1993a) 'Dark and Lovely Too: Black Gay Men in Independent Film', in M. Gever, P. Parmar and J. Greyson (eds) *Queer Looks: Perspectives on Lesbian and Gay Film and Video*. London: Routledge, 238–56.

_____ (1993b) 'Reading Racial Fetishism: The Photographs of Robert Mapplethorpe', in E. Apter and W. Pietz (eds) *Fetishism as Cultural Discourse*. Ithaca: Cornell University Press, 307–29.

Miller, D. A. (1991) 'Anal Rope', in D. Fuss (ed.) *Inside/Out: Lesbian Theories, Gay Theories*. New York: Routledge, 119–41.

_____ (1999) 'Visual Pleasure in 1959', in E. Hanson (ed.) *Outtakes: Essays on Queer Theory and Film*. Durham: Duke University Press, 97–125.

Mulvey, L. (1988a [1975]) 'Visual Pleasure and Narrative Cinema', in C. Penley (ed.) *Feminism and Film Theory*. New York: Routledge, 57–68.

_____ (1988b [1981]) 'Afterthoughts on "Visual Pleasure and Narrative Cinema" inspired by *Duel in the Sun*', in C. Penley (ed.) *Feminism and Film Theory*. New York: Routledge, 69–79.

Munford, R. (2004) '"Wake Up and Smell the Lipgloss": Gender, Generation and the (A)politics of Girl Power', in S. Gillis, G. Howie and R. Munford (eds) *Third Wave Feminism: A Critical Exploration*. New York: Palgrave, 142–53.

Murray, D. (2000) *Bosie: The Man, the Poet, the Lover of Oscar Wilde: A Biography of Lord Alfred Douglas*. New York: Miramax Books.

Ohi, K. (2001) 'Devouring Creation: Cannibalism, Sodomy, and the Scene of Analysis in *Suddenly, Last Summer*', in M. Tinkcom and A. Villarejo (eds) *Keyframes: Popular Cinema and Cultural Studies*. London: Routledge, 259–79.

Oosterhuis, H. (2000) *Stepchildren of Nature: Krafft-Ebing, Psychiatry, and the Making of Sexual Identity*. Chicago: The University of Chicago Press.

Oswald, R. (1990 [1919]) 'Richard Oswald', *Film-Kurier*, 24, n.p., in H. Belach and W. Jacobsen (eds) *Richard Oswald: Regisseur und Produzent*. Munich: edition text + kritik, 33–4.

Parkerson, M. (1993) 'Birth of a Notion: Towards Black Gay and Lesbian Imagery in Film and Video', in M. Gever, J. Greyson, P. Parmar (eds) *Queer Looks: Perspectives on Lesbian and Gay Film and Video*. London: Routledge, 234–7.

Prasch, T. (1993) 'Edward II', *American Historical Review*, 98, 4, 1164–6.

Prinzler, H. H. (ed.) (2003) *Friedrich Wilhelm Murnau: Ein Melancholiker des Films*. Berlin: Stiftung Deutsche Kinemathek.

Rees-Roberts, N. (2008) *French Queer Cinema*. Edinburgh: Edinburgh University Press.

Reinig, C. (1983) 'Christa Reinig über Christa Winsloe', in C. Winsloe, *Mädchen in Uniform*. Munich: Frauenoffensive, 241–8.

Rich, B. R. (1998a) *Chick Flicks: Theories and Memories of the Feminist Film Movement*. Durham: Duke University Press.

____ (1998b [1979–83]) 'From Repressive Tolerance to Erotic Liberation: Maedchen in Uniform', in B. R. Rich, *Chick Flicks: Theories and Memories of the Feminist Film Movement*. Durham: Duke University Press, 179–206.

____ (2004 [1992]) 'New Queer Cinema', in M. Aaron (ed.) *New Queer Cinema: A Critical Reader*. Edinburgh: Edinburgh University Press, 15–22.

Richardson, C. (1995) 'Monika Treut: An Outlaw at Home', in P. Burston and C. Richardson (eds) *A Queer Romance: Lesbians, Gay Men and Popular Culture*. London: Routledge, 167–85.

Rubin, G. (1997 [1975]) 'The Traffic in Women: Notes on the "Political Economy" of Sex', in L. Nicholson (ed.) *The Second Wave: A Reader in*

Feminist Theory. London: Routledge, 27–62.

Russo, V. (1995 [1981]) *The Celluloid Closet*. New York: Quality Paperback Book Club.

Sacher-Masoch, L. v. (1989 [1871]) 'Venus in Furs', in Gilles Deleuze, *Masochism: Coldness and Cruelty*. New York: Zone Books, 143–271.

Schaefer, E. (1999) *Bold! Daring! Shocking! True!: A History of Exploitation Films, 1919–1959*. Durham: Duke University Press.

Schlüpmann, H. and K. Gramann (1981) 'Momente erotischer Utopie – ästhetisierte Verdrängung: Zu *Mädchen in Uniform* und *Anna und Elisabeth*', *Frauen und Film*, 28, 28–31.

Schneider, J. (1997) 'Militarism, Masculinity and Modernity in Germany, 1890–1914', Dissertation, Cornell University.

Schoppmann, C. (ed.) (1991) *Im Fluchtgepäck die Sprache: Deutsch- sprachige Schriftstellerinnen im Exil*. Berlin: Orlanda Frauenverlag.

____ (1996) *Days of Masquerade: Life Stories of Lesbians During the Third Reich*. New York: Columbia University Press.

Sedgwick, E. K. (1985) *Between Men: English Literature and Male Homo- social Desire*. New York: Columbia University Press.

____ (1990) *Epistemology of the Closet*. Berkeley: University of California Press.

Sontag, S. (1999 [1964]) 'Notes on "Camp"', in F. Cleto (ed.) *Camp: Queer Aesthetics and the Performing Subject: A Reader*. Ann Arbor: The University of Michigan Press, 53–65.

Steakley, J. (2007) *'Anders als die Andern': Ein Film und seine Geschichte*. Hamburg: Männerschwarm.

Stearns, P. N. (1995) 'The Culture Wars, 1965–1995: A Historian's Map', *Journal of Social History*, 29, Special Issue: *Social History and the American Political Climate: Problems and Strategies*, 17–37.

Talvacchia, B. (1993) 'Historical Phallicy: Derek Jarman's *Edward II*', *Oxford Art Journal*, 16, 1, 112–28.

Tinkcom, M. (2002) *Working Like a Homosexual: Camp, Capital, Cinema*. Durham: Duke University Press.

Töteberg, M. (1990) 'Warnung vor einer heiligen Nutte oder die sich ver- kaufen', in H. Belach and W. Jacobsen (eds) *Richard Oswald: Regisseur und Produzent*. Munich: edition text + kritik, 113–18.

Truffaut, F. (1985) *Hitchcock*. New York: Simon and Schuster.

Von der Emde, S. (1991) '*Mädchen in Uniform*: Erotische Selbstbefreiung der Frau im Kontext der Kino-Debatte der Weimarer Republik', *Kodikas/ Code: Ars Semiotica*, 14, 35–48.

Von Praunheim, R. (2003) 'Mythos und Legende', in H. H. Prinzler (ed.) *Friedrich Wilhelm Murnau: Ein Melancholiker des Films*. Berlin: Stiftung Deutsche Kinemathek, 132–4.

Wallenberg, L. (2004) 'New Black Queer Cinema', in M. Aaron (ed.) *New Queer Cinema: A Critical Reader*. Edinburgh: Edinburgh University Press, 128–43.

Waters, J. (1995 [1981]) *Shock Value*. New York: Thunder's Mouth Press.

Watson, P. (1997) 'There's No Accounting for Taste: Exploitation Cinema and the Limits of Film Theory', in D. Cartmell, I.Q.Hunter, H. Kaye and I. Whelehan (eds) *Trash Aesthetics: Popular Culture and its Audience*. London: Pluto Press, 66–83.

Weiss, A. (1992) *Vampires and Violets: Lesbians in Film*. New York: Penguin.

White, P. (1999) *unInvited: Classical Hollywood Cinema and Lesbian Representability*. Bloomington: Indiana University Press.

White, R. (2007) 'Introduction: Special Feature on *Brokeback Mountain*', *Film Quarterly*, 60, 3, 20.

Wilton, T. (1995) *Immortal, Invisible: Lesbians and the Moving Image*. London: Routledge.

Winsloe, C. (1930) *Gestern und Heute (Ritter Nerestan)*. Berlin: Georg Marton Verlag.

_____ (1983 [1934]) *Mädchen in Uniform*. Munich: Frauenoffensive.

Wolf, N. (2002 [1991]) *The Beauty Myth: How Images of Beauty Are Used Against Women*. New York City: Harper Perennial.

Zur Nieden, S. (2003) 'Der "kesse Vater" und seine Beziehung zu den "Geschlechtscharakteren"', in B. Duden, K. Hagemann, R. Schulte, U. Weckel (eds) *Geschichte in Geschichten: Ein historisches Lesebuch*. Frankfurt: Campus, 319–24.

INDEX

Lightning Source UK Ltd.
Milton Keynes UK
UKHW010249130223
416873UK00006B/379